Diaspora, Culture and Identity

Diaspora, Culture and Identity

Asian Indians in America

Poonam Bala

RAWAT PUBLICATIONS

Jaipur • New Delhi • Bangalore • Hyderabad • Guwahati • Kolkata

ISBN 978-81-316-0718-3

Published by
Prem Rawat for **Rawat Publications**
Satyam Apts, Sector 3, Jawahar Nagar, Jaipur 302 004 (India)
Phone: 0141 265 1748 / 7006 Fax: 0141 265 1748
E-mail: info@rawatbooks.com
Website: www.rawatbooks.com

New Delhi Office
4858/24, Ansari Road, Daryaganj, New Delhi 110 002
Phone: 011 2326 3290

Also at *Bangalore, Hyderabad, Guwahati* and *Kolkata*

Typeset by Rawat Computers, Jaipur
Printed at Chaman Enterprises, New Delhi

Dedicated to

my father (late) **Raghubir Narain**
and my mother, **Sharda,**
for their inspiration, love and support

Contents

List of Plates

Foreword

During the last quarter of the twentieth century, the nature of immigration to the United States changed dramatically. For most of the nation's history, Europeans dominated the movement of people into the US; their position assured by protective and highly discriminatory legislation passed in the late nineteenth and early twentieth centuries. Passage of a new immigration law in 1965, finally, removed those legal barriers.

Within slightly over a decade, thereafter, the sources of immigration shifted away from Europe. Migrants from Asia, South America, and the Middle East soon formed the majority of the migrant flow – a majority that has continued to grow up to the present. In retrospect, this change was to be expected. The new law came into force during the post-colonial period in Asia and Africa, as well as at a time when economic, technological, and productive changes were taking place throughout the globe. Americans quite suddenly had to re-imagine the nature of immigration in what can now be characterized as the post-Ellis Island era. The faces they saw, the new languages they heard and popular cultural shifts in cuisine and music reflected the more truly global nation they lived in.

The 'new' immigrants who arrived in the United States at this time found themselves, in many instances, as pioneers in a new land with little cultural continuity to that which they had left. That was particularly the story of Asian Indians who arrived in the US. Having come from what had been part of the British Empire they usually brought with them both linguistic skills and an educational background, which would assist in adapting to and working in a new home. Despite this, they were still strangers in a nation that was culturally far distant from that which they had left – religion, food-ways and popular cultural affinities (cricket is not baseball) often separated them from the broader community as did that community's minimal and often misinformed knowledge of India and their new Indian immigrant colleagues and co-workers.

It is this critical pioneer period of encounter and adjustment among early Asian-Indian immigrants to Northeast Ohio that forms the core of *Diaspora, Culture and Identity: Asian Indians in America* by *Poonam Bala*. Her focus on the manner in which these early immigrants dealt with matters of adjustment, accommodation, adoption and acceptance is critical to understanding how the Asian-Indian community in this region, as well as elsewhere in the Asian-Indian diaspora, created functional sub-communities in disparate culture environments.

Today, the Greater Cleveland, Ohio, area has a relatively sizable Asian Indian community. While not as large as those in cities like New York, Chicago and Los Angeles, the community in Northeast Ohio is diverse in terms of regional Indian sub-identities. It is prosperous and very much a part of the medical and research infrastructure of Cleveland's post-industrial past. It is also multi-generational. That aspect of life – the transmission (or lack, thereof) of language, custom and identity, is the component of this study that moves it beyond the pioneer period of settlement and adds immensely to our understanding of both compromise and continuity within and, one can argue, beyond the regional Asian-Indian community. The value of *Diaspora, Culture and Identity: Asian Indians in America* as a scholarly study, therefore, transcends the locality on which it is focused. It also stands as a major contribution to the body of literature documenting migration, identity, and diversity in Northeast Ohio.

John J. Grabowski, Ph.D.
Krieger-Mueller Associate Professor of Applied History
Case Western Reserve University
Senior Vice President for Research and Publications
Western Reserve Historical Society
USA

Acknowledgements

My interest in the South Asian community in Ohio was prompted during my teaching tenure at Case Western Reserve University in Cleveland, Ohio. The insights provided by my students during various class discussions and personal interactions over a span of few years inspired me to undertake a deeper vision of what it meant to be part of a different, yet a connecting, culture in America. However, a successful inquest into this very important, yet an unexplored area, came to fruition when my colleague, John J. Grabowski, invited me to pen all these experiences in a book form. Besides giving me this tremendous opportunity, his timely communication on various issues pertaining to the book, goes a long way in making this study feasible, for which I offer my personal thanks to him. To Alan Rocke, I am grateful for his kind help in getting access to rare library sources, and to a dear friend and colleague, Rhonda Williams, for her enriching discussions and for accommodating my academic requests despite her perpetually busy schedule, my note of appreciation.

I also thank all my students at Case Western Reserve University, and their families, for sharing their experiences as members of the Asian Indian community in Ohio. Without their help in providing the much needed information, this study would not have taken shape. My special thanks to my student, Ashwin Parulkar, for his help in reaching his friends and their families with timely reminders to them about the urgency of the information pertaining to this study.

I am deeply indebted to Paramjit Singh for introducing me to his fellow friends from the Asian Indian community who came to Cleveland in the 1950s and 60s. Despite his busy engagements, he made time to share information, through telephone communication, if not always through personal meetings. Without his help, I would never have been able to reach out to other fellow Asian Indians and I am grateful to him for providing the platform for communicating with other members of the Asian Indian community. Besides, I express my deep sense of gratitude to Dr Ashok Pradhan, Dr Minal Pradhan, Sham Gautam, and Ajeet Singh Sood, Dr Gita Gidwani, Dr Hans Nagpaul and Kamala Nagpaul, for their active participation in this project by sharing their real life experiences as one of the first Asian Indians in Cleveland. I have no words to express my gratitude to Dr Ashok Pradhan and his wife Dr Minal Pradhan for welcoming me to their home for lively conversations and discussions on their rich experiences in Cleveland; in writing this, unfortunately, Dr Minal Pradhan is sadly missed owing to her recent and untimely death.

To Ajeet Singh Sood, I am truly indebted for sharing some of the original documents and personal photographs via long distance communication. He went out of his way to make them accessible within a short span of time and in the most methodical manner despite his daily commitments.

To Phil Manning and the Sociology Department at Cleveland State University, I am especially grateful for extending all academic support. Thanks are also due to the staff at Kelvin Smith and Allen Medical libraries for their help in tracing books at a short notice. To Debra, I am especially grateful for her help in procuring books and to Wendy and other staff at the Lee Public Library, my gratitude for their help in handling difficult imaging issues of original documents. To Ann Holstein, I remain indebted for a meticulous projection of data and mapping.

While this book has long been in the making, it is to Professor Pranav Desai at the Centre for Studies in Science Policy (CSSP), Jawaharlal Nehru University, that I extend my warm gratitude for inviting me as a Visiting Professor – an affiliation which eventually saw the completion of this work and Dr Madhav Govind – thanks for all your support as the new Chairperson; I also offer a note of thanks to other colleagues at CSSP – Saradindu, Krishna, Jayanta, Dinesh and Rajbeer.

Thanks are also due to Pranit Rawat and his editorial team at Rawat Publications for overseeing this project with extreme patience.

Priya, Neelam, Meera, Shuchi, Tasnim and Sangita – I owe you more than I can say here – thank you for your friendship. To my husband, Niraj Varma, my gratitude for the much-needed inspiration and support without which this journey would not have been complete.

Last, but not the least, a special note of appreciation for my mother whose love and inspiration continue to guide me in my academic pursuits and remain, undeniably, consequential.

2015

Poonam Bala

Note on names in the study

The names of the first Asian Indians, as discussed in chapter 3 are real and have been mentioned in the study with their kind permission. However, as requested by some participants, some names in chapter 4 have been altered while others only bear altered initials.

CHAPTER 1

Reflections on Migration of Asian Indians

An Introduction

The recent spur in literature on various aspects of the Asian community in general and Asian Indians in particular, has focused largely on either the changing status of Indian women or on the social and cultural transformations they have undergone as immigrants from a vastly different culture, or on a feminist perspective of Indian women in America.[1] Recent studies have alluded to the Asian Indian immigration in the broader context of Asian immigration to the United States. Most immigrants from India, these studies indicate, were primarily men from the region of Punjab in the northern part of India[2] which detail histories of displacement of, more specifically, the Sikh diaspora. In addition, some studies have focused on the linguistic, cultural and religious ideologies in view of the 'adopted' socio-cultural values amongst the Hindu diaspora across different cultures.[3] Besides, while some studies have brought out discussions on the gendered and class nature of the diasporic communities in general,[4] the past two decades have witnessed the domination of diaspora and transnationalism in migration studies, with a new focus in social science research.[5] More recently, diaspora and migration have occupied a central place in post-colonial thought that allude to concepts of displacement or the politics of dispossession. While both phenomena alter the demographic patterns, as also the cultural compositions, they have ushered in new understandings of displacement or 'belonging' as a post-colonial condition. While explaining these in relation to globalization is important, what is equally significant is the latter's impact on the emergence of diaspora. Thus, understood in terms of its colonial and postcolonial dimensions, globalization offers an understanding of the dissemination of social identities and the circulation of cultural practices. In defining the term diaspora, questions dwelling on the emergence of the diasporas and their discussion in a historical context have been the focus of academic debates. Sometimes, diaspora is understood in reference to 'emigrant communities-populations that originate from a nation-state that is different from the one where they reside.'[6] Other scholars have engaged in conceptualising diaspora as 'encompassing a wider range of originary moments.'[7] Viewed, thus, contemporary works on diaspora are based on the traditional paradigms of immigration patterns studied by sociologists, anthropologists, historians and other scholars. In some cases, while this line of inquiry forms the bulk of explanations of Indian communities abroad, it also offers perspectives on post-colonial migration and hence, on post-structural theories. In this context, the term diaspora evokes a sense of belonging that enables representation of a particular group in the adopted country. It often exemplifies a contact arena within which various forms of identity and national belongingness, are expressed and exhibited. In her recent study on the Indian diaspora in the US, Sahay[8] provides new perspectives on understanding the political and economic benefits of Indian migration to the US. In discussing the role of immigrant entrepreneurs in the development of India, she views diasporic communities as agents of development, focusing on the means by which skills, knowledge and human capital can contribute to positive development and hence, of policy decisions on development strategies.[9] This is a significant two-way process where, as Sahay remarks,

> In an era of globalization, the movement of people (like goods and services) no longer remains unidirectional.[10]

In explaining mobility from this perspective, issues of migration become significant. An important factor influencing migration patterns is the historical linkage between former imperial powers and their colonies of the past in the wake of decolonization.[11] In the period following World War II, these linkages were a result of political, social and cultural ties between the two which led to an 'almost spontaneous mobility'[12] of immigrants between Europe and other cultures; some countries which experienced large-scale migration included Britain, the Netherlands, France and Portugal. Post-colonialism, in this respect, offers new visions and horizons in understanding history from a different perspective. It offers a new paradigm within which the existing political and socio-economic problems, often interpreted as a failure to integrate the immigrant populations into the host society that further exacerbate and complicate problems expressed by the local people, are understood from the point of view of the immigrants.[13] Post-colonialism allows the construction of a framework within which the stories and experiences of the immigrants can be heard and understood from different perspectives – that is, from the perspectives of the immigrants – their decisions and individual choices. The study is situated within this new paradigm enabling an understanding of the narratives and personal trajectories of the Asian Indians that emigrated to Northeast Ohio, for these stories uncover the relationship between the 'lost' self and the social space.[14] As Ashcroft et al. state, a major feature of post-colonial literatures is the crisis of identity and authenticity and for migrants, the recovery of 'an effective identifying relationship between self and space.'[15]

In as much as above perspectives provide answers to various issues about the Asian or Asian Indian diaspora, in general, they fall short in detailing their experiences in relation to issues of identity, social and cultural adjustments and perception of parent cultures by second and third generations in specific regions of America. The book, thus, aims to bridge the literary gap in understanding the social trajectories of the Asian Indians in Northeast Ohio. It is written in the belief that there exists no major work that documents the voices, as also the unspoken and unheard voices, that need to be appreciated, documented and recognized in order to understand the trajectories of the Asian Indian community in Northeast Ohio through, what I call, the four '**A**'s of Asian Indian trajectory – these are represented as **A***djustment,* **A***ccommodation,* **A***doption* and **A***cceptance*. While the process and the establishment of the diasporic community may vary within communities or even the same society, they still form the platform from which emerges an understanding of the diasporic condition. The four '**A**'s, thus, allude to different stages in the process of initial encounters and later a gradual process of absorption into the new social and cultural environment of the host country. The first phase of the trajectory, **A***djustment,* is the most crucial of all phases. Representing a 'maiden' interaction with the new culture, this phase is often marked by a strong sense of 'detachment' and 'distinctness' and perhaps, a 'loss' of traditional ethnic identity. The feeling of 'loss' of identity gradually tapers as the immigrant community gradually **A***ccommodates* the host social and cultural environment that facilitate the establishment and reconstitution of new 'self' within a new social space. In the third phase, while the ethnic institutional and social and cultural networks remain embedded in the visions of the immigrant community, new ones are **A***dopted* in the process. The final trajectory of **A***cceptance* is by no means indicative of the loss of 'identity,' but is a reconstitution of the 'self' or 'becoming' as well as of 'being.'[16] Underlying this trajectory is a belief in shared culture and cultural identity providing a common frame of reference which Hall describes in terms of common historical experiences and shared cultural codes.[17] He also adds,

> 'this "oneness", underlying all the other, more superficial differences, is the truth, ... and a powerful creative force in emergent forms of representation.'[18]

In post-colonial societies, the rediscovery of this identity is often the object of what Fanon[19] once called a passionate research, ... directed by the secret hope of discovering beyond the misery of today, beyond self-contempt, resignation and abjuration, some very beautiful and splendid era whose existence rehabilitates us both in regard to ourselves and in regard to others.[20] While these are unstated voices that need to be addressed, they are part of the immigrant establishments not only in the State of Ohio but also in the entire America – for they have, and still do, played a significant role in the lives of the Asian Indian community in America.

Several reasons have contributed to undertaking this study. My academic trajectories across different parts of the world – United Kingdom, Canada and America – added to this multitude of experiences with a new and different culture, as a student and later a teacher, which facilitated extensive interactions with children of first and second generation Asian Indians in Ohio. Besides, teaching at Case Western Reserve University gave me a real life experience of interacting closely with Asian Indian students over a lengthy span of time. It provided new vistas to uncover issues of identity and social place that the Asian Indian community faced in the American society. These encounters and experiences justified the urgency prompting the need to bring to the reader an interpretative and empirical study documenting these 'unspoken' and significant voices of the Asian Indian community in Ohio.

It has been a privilege to include real life experiences of some of the first Asian Indians who came to Cleveland, for work or higher education, in the 1960s. Their voices have given new perspectives to our understanding of social issues of diversity in a new cultural setting. The study is also based on personal interviews and interactions, in addition to open ended questionnaires sent to students (and their parents) at Case Western Reserve University; some of these were discussed and debated upon in class settings over a period of time, exploring the ways in which personal and collective memories and narratives in the form of 'voices' and opinions, which otherwise have remained obscure, in issues of creating new spaces and identity in a new culture. To this effect,

> ideas about personal memory are closely tied to debates about identity and attempts to situate knowledge, ...[21]

What makes the study more challenging is the contrast between 'what has been passed to these students by their Asian parents,' and 'how much of these cultural aspects have been assimilated by their children.' In trying to find a balance between the two, apparently, issues of a social, ethnic and national identity come to the fore. As a result, a majority of them try to adopt a life style that is more akin to their country of birth – a style that suits them but often conflicts with that of their parents or the culture of their parents. Thus, what is discussed here is the various ways in which the migrant Asian Indian community has negotiated a new life in a new social, cultural and political environment, allowing the creation of imagined communities of nations, by creating identities, and by expressing themselves as multiply constituted.[22]

The study will offer new perspectives in studying other immigrant communities in America. Equally important is the platform this study is hoped to provide in understanding new presentations of the experiences or their differences and similarities in the Asian Indian communities in a global context.

The following chapter provides a historical background of migration patterns in the nineteenth and twentieth centuries, describing the socio-cultural patterns, settlement choices and decisions on perpetuation of social and cultural values. More pertinent are reasons for emigration, which are stated to be economical, better employment, political or social. In as much as these are significant, the adaptive modifications that take place within the new culture require a deeper understanding of how the migrating communities reconstruct their social life. The changes that take place as a result have survived as the memory of lived experiences which form the core of Chapter 3. It is based on the memories documented as significant narratives of some of the first Asian Indians who came to Cleveland and re-established their new social space, intercepted by long phases of personal resignation and acceptance of a new mode of life. In so doing, they have left indelible landmarks which will be treasured by successive generations as a repository of knowledge and experiences.

The following are some of the major landmarks created by Asian Indians in Ohio.[23]

1. Shanti Bahadur, who came in 1949, established the first business of restoring old photographs on East 4th Street (Euclid and Prospect Avenues).
2. Dr Vishwa Nath Kapur was the first Indian physician on the staff of Metro General Hospital.
   The first Sikh doctor interned in Lutheran Hospital.

3. The first Sikh social worker employed by B.F. Goodrich Center in 1960s.
4. The first Indian entertainment program of Indian music and dance held at the Cleveland.
5. The first Indian Republic Day dinner organized in 1963 for 125 people at the International Student Center.
6. Indian Association of Cleveland was formed in 1964.
7. First turbaned Sikh, Ajeet Singh Sood, graduated at the ceremony at Case Institute of Technology in 1963.
8. First turbaned Sikh, Paramjit Singh, graduated at the ceremony at Western Reserve University in 1965.
9. The first Indian newspaper, *Lotus,* published in 1967.
10. First Indian store of Indian handicrafts, jewellery and clothing, started by Paramjit Singh in 1968, on Coventry Road, Cleveland Heights.
11. The first Indian grocery store opened in the Greenlight Shopping Mall in the second half of 1960s.
12. Taj Mahal, is the first Indian restaurant opened in Lyndhurst in 1974.
13. The growth of the Indian community in the early 1970s inspired the establishment of an India House which later developed into the India Community Center in 1978. By this, Cleveland became the first city in the United States to have an *India Community Center,* receiving the Ohio Historical Marker in 2003.
14. *The Federation of India Community Associations* (FICA) was formed in 1981. It linked up with *The National Federation of Indian-American Associations* (NFIA) thereby serving as the umbrella for all sister organizations.
15. With an increase in the number of physicians moving to Ohio, the foundation of the first *Asian-Indian Physicians of Northern Ohio* (AIPNO) in 1983 was an important change in the community awareness of recognizing skilled and qualified members. The association organizes an annual fund-raising event, *Chirag* (Lamp) which, since 1992, has

donated about $ 10,000 to various non-profit organizations in Ohio. Prominent amongst these include The Free Clinic, Cleveland Sight Center, Templum House, Providence House, Boys Hope, Help Foundation, Inc., Cleveland Sight Center, Center for Provision of Domestic Violence, Cystic Fibrosis Foundation-Rainbow Chapter and The Leukemia and Lymphoma Society.

16. Regular health fairs for seniors are also organized at the *Shiva Vishnu* and *Swaminarayan* temples. AIPNO has also been active in supporting various relief events in India including medical and surgical camps, Burn Clinic in India, Gujarat Earthquake Relief, Orissa Cyclone Relief, India Cultural Garden Project and Tsunami and Hurricane Katrina relief (through Red Cross).[24]
17. Several cultural events have been organized to maintain 'cultural contacts' with India. In 1988, the *Global Organization of People of Indian Origin* (GOPIO) was formed. Besides, the *Asian-Indian Americans for Better Government* (AIABG) is a non-profit organization responsible for educating the community in politics and to raise funds for its participation in politics. Jay Goyal is the first Indian to become the Ohio State Representative.
18. Poonam Bala, who taught South Asian history at Case Western Reserve University, was the first Indian to speak at the *City Club of Cleveland* at a debate between India and Pakistan on 'The Kashmir Dilemma,' on 25 September 2002 (as per the City Club Speakers Master List).
19. The first Gandhi statue in Ohio was installed on 1 October 2006.
20. Monte Ahuja made a generous contribution of $30 million to the University Hospital of Cleveland in 2007.
21. Paramjit Singh is the first Indian to be inducted to the Inaugural Class of Cleveland International Hall of Fame at a ceremony held on 12 May 2010.

India possesses a unique culture where traditional customs and institutions remain paramount in providing social directions to her people. Amongst these, arranged marriages and caste system constitute significant and integral elements of the Indian society. Ironically, despite the shortcomings inherent in arranged marriages, or with hierarchy and social inequalities inherent in the caste system, both have survived not only in the Indian society but have also become the sojourners to the Indian diaspora. Besides, issues of language of different regions in India also reveal the diversity in Indian culture. Chapter 4, thus, identifies some of these issues in detail to understand how the institutional transfer from the parent country to America has survived amidst new cultural patterns. It examines arranged marriage as an institution which can sometimes be an impediment to developing constructive relations between first and second generation members of the Indian community. Conflicting issues emerge when the latter identify themselves with the American culture and life style. Consequently, the Asian Indian community, including the first and second generations, tend to explore the institutional veracity levels, alongside issues of rejection, non-acceptability or acceptability in a different form. New perspectives will be added to this discussion with views on gender issues and more particularly, how women are perceived by the Asian Indian community. The study concludes with an understanding of the trajectories of the Asian Indian community in Northeast Ohio incorporating new forms of identity in the process. Besides proving significant to scholars, researchers and students of international studies, social sciences, politics of migration, the study will encourage further research and a deeper insight into social and cultural issues in forming new identities in the process of *Adjustment, Accommodation, Adoption* and *Acceptance* of new cultures by the diverse Asian Indian community in a global context.

Notes

1. Chitra Banerjee Divakaruni, 2001, *Arranged Marriages: Stories*, New York: Anchor Books, 1995.
2. Karen Isaksen Leonard, 1997, *The South Asian Americans*, Westport: Greenwood Press.
3. See Bhiku Parekh, Gurharpal Singh and Steven Vertovec (eds), 2005, *Culture and Economy in the Indian Diaspora*, London and New York: Routledge.
4. See for example, Vijay Agnew (ed.), 2005, *Diaspora, Memory, and Identity: A Search for Home*, Toronto: University of Toronto Press.
5. See Rainer Bauböck and Thomas Faist (eds), 2010, *Diaspora and Transnationalism: Concepts, Theories and Methods*, IMISCOE Research: Amsterdam University Press.
6. Latha Varadarajan, 2010, *The Domestic Abroad: Diasporas in International Relations*, Oxford: Oxford University Press, 8.
7. See Robin Cohen, *Global Diasporas*, cited by Latha Varadarajan, *The Domestic Abroad*, p. 8. Diaspora is also a multidisciplinary field enriched by the works of anthropologists, psychoanalysis, post-structuralist theorists historians, and literary studies. Seminal writings include those by Homi Bhabha, Gayatri Chrabarty Spivak, Stuart Hall, Paul Arjun Appadurai, and Jacques Derrida.
8. Anjali Sahay, 2009, *Indian Diaspora in the United States: Brain Drain or Gain?*, Lanham: Lexington Books, p. viii.
9. Ibid., 9.
10. Ibid., 10.
11. Thomas Faist, 2000, *The Volume and Dynamics of International Migration and Transnational Social Spaces*, Oxford: Oxford University Press.
12. For details, see Theodoros Iosifides, 2011, *Qualitative Methods in Migration Studies: A Critical Realist Perspective*, Surrey:Ashgate Publishing Limited, 9–10.
13. Fanon and Spivak, the leading proponents of postcolonial studies.
14. See Bill Ashcroft, Gareth Griffiths and Helen Tiffin (eds),1989, *The Empire writes back*, London: Routledge, 9.
15. Ibid.

16. Stuart Hall, 1990, 'Cultural Identity and Diaspora' in J. Rutherford (ed.), *Identity, Community, Culture and Difference*, London: Lawrence and Wishart, 222–37, 225.
17. Ibid., 223.
18. Ibid.
19. Frantz Fanon, 1963, 'On National Culture,' in Frantz Fanon, *The Wretched of the Earth* (trans.RichardPhilcox), New York: Grove Press,170. See also Hall, ibid.
20. see Hall, 'Cultural Identity and Diaspora,' 223.
21. See Edward Said, 2005, 'Out of Place: A Memoir, London: Granta' in Alison Blunt, *Domicile and Diaspora: Anglo-Indian Women and the Spatial Politics of Home*, Massachussetts: Blackwell Publishing, 13.
22. Sandhya Shukla, 2003, *India Abroad: Diasporic Cultures of Post-war America and England*, New Jersey: Princeton University Press, 4.
23. Federation of India Community Associations (FICA). 2006–07, 'What our Indian-ness offers the World,' Annual Report, (Cleveland: Federation of Indian Community Associations of NE Ohio. 20–22; some entries not updated listed in the Report yet).
24. FICA Annual report, ibid., 21.

CHAPTER 2

Travels Across

Asian Indians in America

The trajectory and motives for emigration of different communities to America as well as globally, over the past three centuries display an immense social and racial diversity of migrant movements. They also allude to the myriad reasons which inspired them to travel across to a new social and cultural environment. Amongst these, the most prominent were economical, grounded in the hope of accumulating quick wealth and commercial rewards. International migration was, however, at its zenith between 1830 and 1930, marked by the migration of workers to the economically advanced nations. This led to an increased social, cultural and political dislocation at both ends.[1] There is, however, a difference in the structural adjustments by Indian communities in the colonial and post-colonial times. While for those who emigrated from India during the colonial period, issues of

> isolation and questions of cultural continuity epitomized their predicament. First within the colonies and then within the successor nation-states, the emigrants remained separate,

> disenfranchised and frequently racialized. In these conditions, successive generations tried to reproduce as accurately as they could the cultural ways of their forbears, while the restrictions on travel as well as the lowly economic status of most overseas Indians limited regular contacts with the 'motherland.'[2]

Migration of Indian communities in the post-independence era, after 1947, enabled better ties with India as a result of new communication technologies that facilitated cultural flow and exchange through transnational networks at home and abroad.

The first group of Indian immigrants to North America in the late nineteenth and early twentieth centuries was primarily drawn from the agricultural areas of the north-western State of Punjab who were involved in lumbering and railway construction in western Canada and the north-western part of America. Over the next few decades, these early immigrant communities became affluent farm owners, with their successive generations settled in the States of Colorado and Texas.[3] The post-1965 US immigration laws and the agricultural restructuring in the aftermath of the Green Revolution increased the influx of Punjabi Sikh immigrants to America. While economic, social or religious reasons guided this movement, migration to new social situations is to be seen as a dynamic process which entailed reconstructing symbols, meanings and definitions to adapt to a new environment.[4] Thus, a majority of the Indian immigrants, who now also comprise a majority of the Asian Indian population in America, came after 1965. Lessinger[5] mentions that the

> continued flow of migration is suggested by the fact that between 55 and 70 per cent of those listing themselves as 'Indians of Asian origin' in the 1990 US Census were born in India.[6]

The process of migration is believed to have led to the emergence of the diaspora, regarded as an almost international phenomenon with a global presence in over 100 countries around the world. Over the last few decades, the term diaspora has been increasingly used by various scholars, intellectuals and political leaders to describe a community that has a 'history of migration.'[7] Shuval[8] offers a lucid explanation of the term diaspora as being

> a social construct founded on feeling, consciousness, memory, mythology, history, meaningful narratives, group identity, longings, dreams, allegorical and virtual elements all of which play an important role in establishing a diaspora reality. At a given moment in time, the sense of connection to a homeland must be strong enough to resist forgetting, assimilating or distancing.

With a long history of migration of the diaspora communities globally, former discourses on concepts of assimilation and immigration have been enriched by new perspectives of trans-nationalism. In this respect, diaspora communities

> serve as exemplary communities of the transnational moment, where the diaspora cultures go beyond and challenge the national boundaries.[9]

With a rich and varied cultural heritage connected with India, the Indian diaspora exhibits a multitude of spatial locations as well as a predominant heterogeneity in terms of language, religion and regional variations in its parent country. Nevertheless, family values and kinship ties continue to play a significant role in the lives of the diaspora communities globally, thus portraying the history of Asian communities as

> one of accommodation to the prevailing historical situation.[10]

In his illuminating selection of writings,[11] the Nobel prize-winning economist, Amartya Sen, discusses the rich intellectual and cultural heritage that India has possessed as one of the world's oldest civilizations, that goes a long way in the making of the contemporary and thriving democracy of today. Viewed thus, he remarks that the existence of a large diaspora abroad also reflects a part of India's interactive presence. While,

> ideas as well as people have moved across India's borders over thousands of years, they have also enriched India as well as the rest of the world. Throughout history, Indians and the Indian diaspora have resisted external isolation as well as internal miniaturization.[12]

The plural and a dynamic heritage have contributed to this process.[13] The liberalization policies in India in the early 1990s, provided new impetus to understanding Indians abroad, initially viewed largely for their economic investment into the subcontinent. Although, continued efforts were made to connect with Indian communities globally, the term diaspora was deployed only after 1994 when an International Conference on Diaspora was organized by the University of Hyderabad in India. The recognition of Indians abroad, their contributions and social and cultural investments into India resulted in the establishment of a Centre for the Study of the Indian Diaspora.[14] Viewed thus, the transference and reconstitution of cultural patterns and social relations in new setting, have been one that usually involves the migrants as minorities becoming set apart by 'race,' language, cultural traditions and religion. Diaspora, in this context, claims Marienstras,[15] refers to especially as an imagined connection between a post-migration (including refugee) population and a place of origin and with people of similar cultural origins elsewhere. By 'imagined,' he does not imply that such connections might not be actual but rather, they emphasize the often strong sentiments and mental pictures according to which members of diasporas organize themselves and undertake their cultural practices. This leads him to view diaspora as a group based on 'a degree of national, or cultural, or linguistic awareness' of 'a relationship, territorially discontinuous, with a group settled elsewhere' that also involves an ongoing exchange of information, money and resources – as well as regular travel and communication.[16]

The Asian Indian Community in Northeast Ohio

The strong presence and establishment of the Indian community are visible globally. Pandit Jawaharlal Nehru, the first Prime Minister of independent India, had once remarked that wherever Indians go, they take a piece of India with them. In a special address,[17] Pranab Mukherjee (former Finance Minister of India), drew attention to the contributions made by the Indian community not only to America but also to the world:

> It is indeed a matter of great pride for us that we represent a great and composite civilization that defines our 'Indian-ness' and our world view. Our thinking is shaped by a history in which practically all the communities of the world have thrived. India has always been a mosaic of cultures and an open society. Great religions have been born in our nation, and many from outside have been absorbed and internalized … . This rich heritage, became an integral part of our identity. In a world of conflict and bigotry, India provides an alternative model of peaceful co-existence.[18]

While relatively few Asian Indians left India in the nineteenth century, a major wave was seen in the first half of the twentieth century. This was a significant movement of Asian Indians, a majority of whom remained concentrated primarily on the west coast in California. The number of immigrants, however, declined with the exclusion of people of Asian origin in the immigration bills of 1917 and 1924 which made it difficult for the settlers of the early twentieth century to possess land rights and American citizenship. It was not until 1946 that some of these stringent laws were relaxed in favor of naturalization of early Asian Indians.[19]

The historical trajectory and the current social demographics of the Asian Indian community in Northeast Ohio, in the city of Cleveland, reflect the settlement pattern not only locally but also for other cities and States in the US, demonstrated by the gradual increase in the number of immigrants coming from different parts of India. Besides India, some 20,000 new immigrants from each country in South Asia came to America after 1965.[20] These movements went alongside cultural and commercial changes in Cleveland – changes which went a long way in marking Cleveland as a city with

> an interesting and diverse history.[21]

Grabowski and Grabowski in their path-breaking study on the history of Cleveland, put into perspective various transportation technologies and connections that went into the making of Cleveland and Northeast Ohio's thriving communities. In other words, their work portrays the history of Cleveland

> that has been put in motion by people, a few famous, some known to a small cadre of historians, and the majority remembered.[22]

This makes a compelling case for the growth of Cleveland and Northeast Ohio and the diverse communities over the past century (Plate 1). Who were these people, who were these communities that comprised an indispensable component of the developing city?

Plate 1

Map indicating the location of the State of Ohio within the United States of America

Map courtesy of Ann Holstein, Freedman Center for Digital Scholarship, Case Western Reserve University (07/15/13)

> Immigrants, entrepreneurs, politicians and professionals set Cleveland and its history in motion. Whether celebrating or struggling, everyday people etched their stories into the city's landscapes – its roads, buildings, bridges and statues. They built the city's infrastructure, developed neighborhoods, and produced the goods that drove the region's economy, all the while creating families and communities.[23]

It is believed that some of the early Asian Indians settled in Cleveland as early as the 1920s, most of whom were students. In the 1930s, however, the number increased to a meager 100 with not much increase in the 1960s when only 169 Indians were living in Cleveland. The movement of Asian Indians to Cleveland, as in the rest of the US, took place in three distinct phases – pre-1965, 1965–1980 and post-1980. Overall, the majority arrived in the US between 1965 and 1980. Their numbers increased from approximately 3,50,000 in 1980 to about 8,00,000 in 1990, with 17,00,000 recorded in the 2000 Census.[24] The 1960s, however, witnessed several changes in the movement of the immigrant communities, especially from the Indian subcontinent. Overall, as reported by Kundu,

> there has been a growing concentration of international out-migrants from Asia in a few countries in the developed world. While In 1960, 57 per cent of all migrants lived in the less developed regions but by 2005, just 37 per cent did so, Asia accounting for 53 million or 28 per cent, basically due to its high demographic weight.[25]

More specifically, the new US immigration laws of 1965 gave precedence to migrant communities with advanced education, professional training or substantial capital to invest. As a result,

> Indian scientists, engineers, medical personnel, financers, entrepreneurs and a host of other professionals began to

> arrive, recruited to fill perceived labor shortages in the ranks of American science and medicine.[26]

After 1967, skilled professionals had a chance to come to America – an opportunity which was restricted in earlier years. So also in Northeast Ohio, the movement of Indian immigrants was set off in the early 1960s when immigration laws had a very limited quota for people from India and Pakistan. However, work opportunities were very attractive to Indians with advanced professional and technical education as a result of which more got inspired and were pulled to the

> well-paid jobs, more rewarding careers and a higher standard of living in the US.[27]

Anand Giridharadas, a noted columnist for the *International Herald Tribune,* and author, in his recent debut book, *India Calling: An Intimate Portrait of a Nation's Remaking,* portrays the changing image of India over the last four decades – the land which his parents left in the 1970s for better professional opportunities in America. Revisiting India, Anand Giridharadas is struck by the social and cultural changes in India – changes that indicate the new India and the new perceptions of people who do not think that they have to leave the country for betterment. He recalls,

> family was the only community that had mattered in India. In America, my parents discovered the community itself. The people who had shared recipes, gave them rides, taught them the idioms they didn't know, brought them food when they were sick. It was perhaps, the grace of this welcome that inoculate them against the defensiveness and nostalgia that so many that so often infect immigrants.[28]

The number of Asian Indians gradually displayed a steep rise, recording up to 2,216 in 1980, and by the following decade, the population in Northeast Ohio had more than doubled, to 5,780. Most of these immigrants were drawn from a group of skilled population including physicians and engineers employed in the medical institutions and corporate organizations in Cleveland, who could find an easy market for their professional skills. This move was also guided by the concomitant emergence of the health care sector and of global transportation in Cleveland so that by the 1970s, the health sector in Cleveland was constituted largely of the immigrant professionals.[29]

Even in the 1970s, a small number of Indian immigrants, about 307, were recorded in Northeast Ohio. However, rules became stringent towards the 1980s when several Indian students stayed on permanently after completing their education in an American university. In Northeast Ohio (in Cleveland), the movement of young students from India and Pakistan followed in the 1960s when a lot of them came on a trainee visa. The dramatic increase in the number of Indian residents in Cleveland also followed the Naturalization Act of 1965 which rescinded restrictive immigration measures that earlier dissuaded immigration into the country. It also established a system that required professional skills as well as reunification of families already resident in Cleveland.

The establishment of medical institutions and hospitals in Cleveland, funded by private and philanthropic enthusiasts coupled with a thriving industrial economy brought Cleveland's medical centers to international fame. Besides, the availability of jet transport facilitated less cumbersome means of treating patients from around the world, who visited the city to receive world-class health care in cardio-thoracic surgery, cardiology, oncology and other specialties.[30] Cleveland, thus, came to be recognized not only for its quality health care provisions that won international repute, but also gained worldwide popularity in terms of training and education in medicine. Alongside the reputed hospitals, Cleveland became a home to immigrants who desired quality higher education. Thus,

> nowhere was the link between higher education and industry closer than on the campus that stood next to but separate from Western Reserve's during the years 1885 to 1967.[31]

Despite the existence of an almost uniform pattern in the professional demographics of the Indian community who came and settled in Northeast Ohio, most members of the Indian community came from different regions in India. However, the most prominent and the maximum number represented the western State of Gujarat in India. According to the *Encyclopedia of Cleveland History*,[32] the early Indian immigrant populations settled mainly in the eastern suburbs of Cleveland Heights and Shaker Heights both of which provided proximity to Cleveland's medical educational institutions (Plate 2). Besides, the new immigrant population from India in Cleveland gradually became visible, with a few Sikhs wearing turbans (religious head gear) in these areas. In the 1970s and 1980s, Asian Indians began to settle in the western suburbs as well, so that by the mid-1980s it was estimated that about 60 per cent of the Indian population lived in the eastern suburbs, and 40 per cent in the western suburbs. Approximately 3,000 Asian Indians were reported in Cleveland in 1990.[33] Between 1965 and 1980, the majority of Asian Indians arriving in Cleveland were educated professionals. While some came to work as engineers in the prosperous industries in Cleveland, others came to train in the engineering and business professions. Besides, women who came at that time were from urban centers in India.[34] With the visibility of Asian Indians in Cleveland, the traditional attire of the Indian community also became noticeable. It was not unusual to see women in their traditional attires (*salwar kameez* and *sari*), while turbaned Sikh men also were seen in Cleveland. Sham Gautam,

Plate 2

Map indicating the residential location of some of the first Asian Indians in north-east Ohio

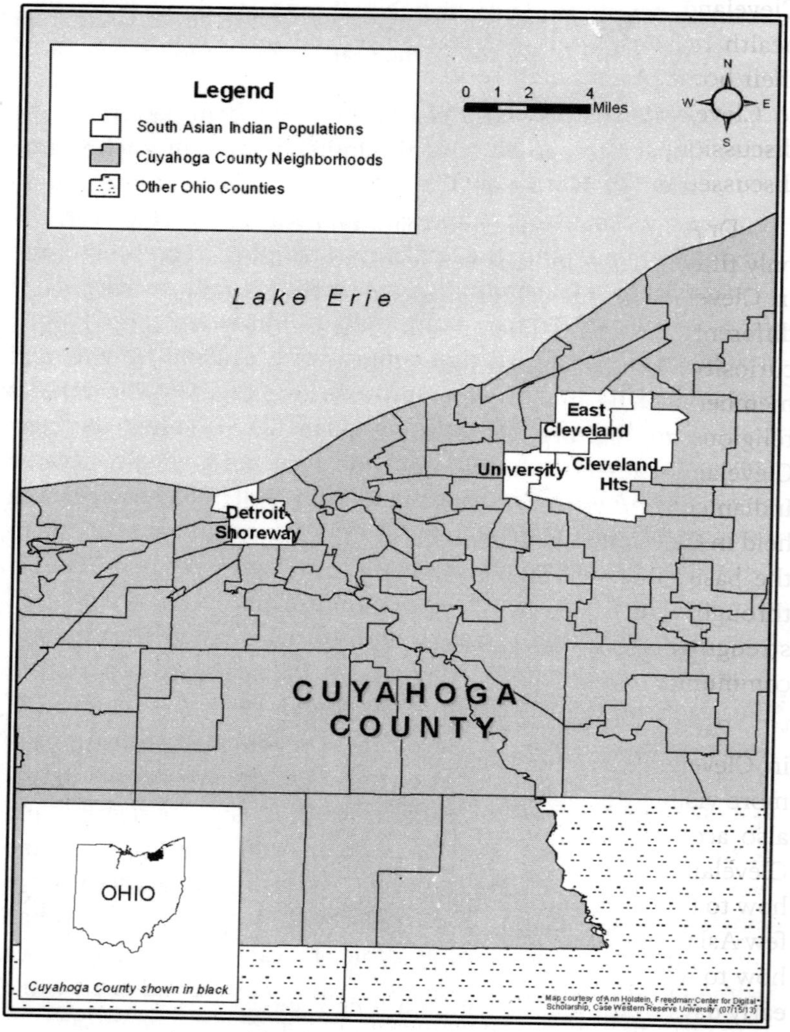

Dr Ashok Pradhan, Dr Minal Pradhan, Gurbaksh Singh, Ajeet Singh Sood, Paramjit Singh, Dr Gita Gidwani, and Kamala Nagpaul are amongst the first (known) Asian Indians to come to Cleveland. Of these, Gurbaksh Singh went back to India for health reasons, while the rest stayed on and made Cleveland their home. Ajeet Singh Sood was one of the first Sikhs to come to Cleveland in 1960, followed by Paramjit Singh in 1962. A discussion of their experiences and career trajectories will be discussed in the next chapter.

Dr Ashok Pradhan recalls that in the early 1960s, there were only fifteen Asian Indians in Cleveland. While cultural visibility in Cleveland in the 1970s made local residents anxious about different cultures, deliberate efforts were made to address this curiosity. As a result, various clubs and organizations invited members of the Indian community to share aspects of Indian religions and culture. Of the first Asian Indians who came to Cleveland, the Sikhs, as the majority were active in promoting Indian cultural visibility. This was done through various events held in Cleveland where members of the Sikh community shared the basic tenets of Sikh philosophy. It also formed a medium through which bonds of cohesion could be visualized and strengthened between the Asian Indians and the local Cleveland community.

Paramjit Singh spoke about Sikhism at various local events in Cleveland. As the social presence of Asian Indians became more visible through these social events, sharing Indian culture also acquired prominence in Cleveland. On one occasion, the Cleveland Play House invited Paramjit Singh to demonstrate how to tie a turban to an invited audience at a play. Likewise, the few Asian Indian women at the time were invited to demonstrate how to wear a sari, the traditional Indian attire. Reminiscing his early days in Cleveland, Paramjit Singh remarks

> we were also treated as guests and given free admission to drive-in movies and putt-putt golf.[35]

Thus, while several Asian Indians from different regions of India came and settled in Cleveland, they often represented pluralistic identities, which were shaped by a multitude of ethnic values of the various social groups. Besides, they also represented and perpetuated

> a recollecting identification with a fictitious or far away existent geographic territory and its cultural-religious traditions.[36]

The notion of social space or 'place' and its links with 'identity' are indispensable to a better understanding of the 'self'. While these are formed during the process of adjustment to the new place, new networks and relations, formed as a result, remain essential components of the manner in which notions of 'place' are perceived and re-constructed by the immigrant communities. What is equally significant is the place they occupy in individuals' lives acquiring special meanings in the context of immigrant communities, for they facilitate and impact upon how

> relationships and social networks are created and maintained, how heritage is understood, reconceived and rewritten, how everyday life is anchored by a strong sense of self , and how narratives and histories are located in time and space.[37]

In the context of identities, Miller remarks that

> immigrant communities bear identities that are in many ways liminal, betwixt and between, no longer of old places yet not fully of new. The certainty that derives from ongoing, intimate experiences of even the varied locales and shifting dispositions of one's homeland-of-identification is absent and the immigrant is left to embrace symbols, to build utopias.[38]

Although, issues of 'place', 'homeland' and the self that nurtured 'new identities' will be discussed in the following chapter, it will be significant at this stage to introduce the reader to the initial engagements of the Asian Indian community in Ohio and in their efforts to negotiate the new 'self' through social and cultural manifestations. One such expression was religion, which is crucial for an understanding of the dynamics of diaspora for it reflects upon collective identity and collective consciousness in the homeland as well as in the new home. In several studies on the dynamics of immigrant settlement and incorporation of new social and cultural elements, religion occupies a salient position, often marked by modifications in its practice within the new settlement processes.[39] Illustrations (Plate 3 and 4) indicate the initial stages of settlement of the Sikh community when explaining the tenets of Sikh philosophy meant a reaffirmation of their religious belonging and collective identity within the new social space. This should also be understood in the context of 'diasporic duality of continuity and change,' – continuity in terms of an identity of belonging and change in terms of the various organizational modifications in the way religion is organized and practiced,[40] grounded in a distinct culture and history at the same time shaped by American experience.

The Indo-Chinese War in 1962 mobilized the Asian Indian community of Cleveland to work with the Cleveland Council on World Affairs to raise funds to support India against Chinese aggression by organizing an entertainment program at the Cleveland Institute of Music sharing Indian songs, music and dances. They were able to raise several thousand dollars that were sent to the Indian Embassy. This also prompted volunteers of the Cleveland Council on World Affairs to invite members of the Asian Indian community to organize social events. Paramjit Singh organized the first Republic Day Dinner in 1963 which also allowed Clevelanders to have their first taste of Indian

Plate 3

Indians give explanation of Sikh Religion
(The Cleveland Press, 17 May 1965; from the personal collection of Ajeet Singh Sood-personal communication)

THE CLEVELAND PRESS, Monday, May 17, 1965 PAGE F 5

Indians Give Explanation of Sikh Religion

By DAVID PIKE

Fifty Greater Clevelanders today have a better understanding of the customs and belief of Sikhism, an Indian religion which has 8,000,000 followers.

Dressed in turbans and beards, the seven members of Cleveland's Sikh community explained and demonstrated their customs and served a dinner of Indian food Saturday night at the Church of the Covenant, 11205 Euclid Ave.

"Sikhism, an attempt to unify religion in India, was founded in Punjab in 1469," explained Pritam Singh Bhatia, a neighborhood worker at West Side Community House.

"Sikhism, which combined parts of the Moslem and Hindu religions, is anti-caste, democratic in organization and holds a belief in one God," Bhatia said. "The religion, about 8 million strong, has as its central concept the universal brotherhood."

HE EXPLAINED that the turban, beard, long hair and bracelet worn by Sikhs were adopted to give the movement a new spirit and identity during a period of persecution. All Sikhs also have the same middle name, Singh.

"The reason for this Sikh "Dewan" or service is the desire to inform others about our culture and customs," said Ajeet Singh Sood, a civil engineer.

We are constantly being asked if we are magicians, Arabians, Russian priests or genies," Bhatia said.

In his introduction, Sood said the Sikhs would like to form an organization and have a meeting place where they can communicate with the public about their religion and customs.

"SUCH A GROUP has been formed in Washington, D. C." he said. " But the Cleveland Public Library has a collection of books on Sikhism," he added.

Anyone wishing to learn about Sikhism or plans for a Cleveland Sikh organization should call Bhatia at PR 1-7297.

Novelist Vailland Dies

BOUR EN BRESSE, France —(UPI)—Roger Vailland, 57, noted French journalist, prize-winning novelist and playwright, died of lung cancer at his home in Meillonas, in Eastern France.

Plate 4

Indians explain Sikh Philosophy (The Plain Dealer, 22 May 1965; from the personal collection of Ajeet Singh Sood)

Indians Explain Sikhs' Philosophy

By FAITH CORRIGAN

The Sixteenth Century, which saw the works of Martin Luther in Germany, was also the period of development of another Protestant religion in the Far East.

Last week at the Church of the Covenant (Presbyterian), 11205 Euclid Avenue, a small band of Indians explained the philosophy of the Sikhs, or Disciples, a religion founded by a spiritual genius, Guru Nanak.

India at the time was divided between two greatly dissimilar faiths, the Moslems and the Hindus. Nanak tried to unite the two into one great brotherhood. He repudiated Hindu idolatry and superstition in favor of one God known as Sat Nam (true name.) Transmigration of the soul, which meant for millions of poverty stricken people that life was an endless curse, was accepted in part, but Nanak taught that salvation could be attained by good works and thus life could accomplish its purpose in one man's period of allotted years.

ANOTHER REVOLUTIONARY idea advanced by Sikhism was equality of women. Marriage is by mutual consent.

"The concept of the priesthood was changed to allow the development of family life," explained Ajeet S. Sood, a graduate of Case Institute of Technology and an engineer with Trygvie Hoff and Associates. Today the religion is administered by committees of laymen and has no central ecclesiastical head.

Most of the seven Sikhs in Cleveland have "Singh" as part of their name. It stands for Lion, a title assumed by more than half of the eight million followers of the faith who are known as keshadharis, or the "hairy ones."

TODAY IN Cleveland, a little six-year-old long haired boy, Jasjeet S. Sood, continues this tradition in the school yard of East Cleveland's Superior School.

Sood is the only Sikh to have his family with him in Cleveland. For this reason he does not suffer from the homesickness that deeply afflicts Harbans S. Sandhu, a University of Michigan graduate and also an engineer with Trygve Hoff and Associates.

"I cannot smile," he said when his picture was being taken by a Plain Dealer photographer. "I have been away from home for four years and three months."

SANDHU HAS surprised several American hostesses when he insists upon washing the dishes after a dinner party.

"To make things clean is my way of praying to God," he explains.

Pritain S. Bhatia is the only one of his fellow churchmen here who is not an engineer. He has his master's degree in social work from the University of Michigan, and is well known on the West Side of Cleveland where he is a member of the staff of the West Side Community House.

BHATIA GAVE the discourse on the principles of Sikhism at the first Dewan held in Cleveland last week. The Dewan, which means "congregation" was attended by 50 Cleveland friends of the Sikh community. For most of them it was their first exposure to a special Eastern heritage of manliness, industry, honesty and pride.

The only student in the group is Paramjit Singh who is working for his master's degree in engineering at Western Reserve University. He is not related to Ranjit Singh, although the names are similar. The latter is a structural engineer with the H. K. Ferguson Co. Another Sikh, Harmohan S. Sethi is also employed by the same Cleveland company.

Jogindar S. Dhillon is the only Sikh to have abandoned the hairy tradition in deference to American ways. But this is not held against him by the other Sikhs who practice the tolerance they preach. A large number of Sikhs in India, the sehjdharis do not have long hair. Dhillon, also a University of Michigan alumus, is a mechanical engineer with the Austin Company.

cuisine and in 1968, he opened the first Indian handicraft store in partnership with five friends from India; the store called *The Maharani*, was located on Coventry Road in Cleveland Heights.

There is much that remains to be known about their real life experiences – experiences which created new landmarks in our understanding of the dynamics of constructing cultural identities in Northeast Ohio. This forms the subject matter of the subsequent chapter.

Notes

1. J.M. Jensen, 1988, *Passage from India: Asian Indian Immigrant in North America*, New Haven: Yale University Press. See also Arpana Sircar, 2000, *Work Role, Gender Roles and Asian Indian Immigrant Women in the United States*, Lewison, New York: The Edwin Mellen Press.
2. Gurharpal Singh, 2003, 'Introduction,' in Bhikhu Parekh, Gurharpal Singh, and Steven Vertovec (eds), *Culture and Economy in the Indian Diaspora*, London: Routledge, 1–12, 5.
3. See details in Johanna Lessinger, 2005, 'Indian Immigrants in the United States: the emergence of a transnational population,' in Bhiku Parekh, Gurharpal Singh and Steven Vertovec (eds), *Culture and Economy in the Indian Diaspora*, London and New York: Routledge, 165–82.
4. Charles E. Waddell and Glenn M Vernon, 1981, 'Ethnic Identity and National Identification: The Social Construction of Commitment of Indian Immigrants to Australia,' in Vinson H. Sutlive, Nathan Altshuler et al. (eds), *Migration and Modernization: The Indian Diaspora in Comparative Perspective* (Studies in Third World Societies), 13–23, 21.
5. Lessinger in Parekh et al. (eds), 2005, 171.
6. S. Galland T. Gall (eds),1993,*Statistical Record of Asian Americans*, Detroit: Gale Research Inc.
7. See R. Marienstrass, 1998. 'On the Notion of Diaspora,' in G. Chaliand (ed.), *Minority Peoples in the Age of Nation-States*, London: Pluto.

8. Judith T. Shuval, 2000, 'Diaspora Migration: Definitional Ambiguities and a Theoretical Paradigm,' *International Migration,* 38(5): 41–56, 43.
9. Khachig Tololyan, 1991,*The Nation State and its Others: In Lieu of a Preface, Diaspora,* 1 (1), 3–7.
10. Dharam P. Ghai and Yash P. Ghai, 1965, 'Asians in East Africa: Problems and Prospects,' *The Journal of Modern African Studies,* 3, 35–51, 5.
11. Amartya Sen, 2005, *The Argumentative Indian: Writings on Indian History, Culture and Identity,* London: Allen Lane, 86.
12. Ibid.
13. Ibid.
14. Parvati Raghuram and Ajay Kumar Sahoo,2008, 'Thinking 'Indian Diaspora' for Our Times,' in Parvati Raghuram and Ajay Kumar Sahoo et al. (eds),*Tracing an Indian Diaspora: Contexts, Memories, Representations,* New Delhi: Sage, 1–20, 7.
15. Richard Marienstras, 1989, 'On the Notion of Diaspora,' in G. Chaliand (ed.), *Minority Peoples in the Age of Nation-States,* London: Pluto, pp. 119–25.
16. Ibid., 120.
17. Reception hosted by the Indian Ambassador to the US in Ohio in 2007.
18. 'What our Indian-ness offers the World,' Federation of India Community Associations (FICA), Annual Report, (Cleveland: Federation of Indian Community Associations of NE Ohio, 4 March 2007), 11.
19. Kirin Narayan, 2004, 'Haunting Stories: Narrative Transmissions and South Asian Diaspora,' in Knut A. Jacobse and P. Pratap Kumar (eds), *South Asians in the Diaspora: Histories and Religious Traditions,* Leiden: Brill, 415–34, 417.
20. Ibid.
21. John J. Grabowski and Diane Ewart Grabowski, 2000, *Cleveland: A History in Motion,* California: Heritage Media Corporation, 12.
22. Ibid., 13.
23. Ibid., 19.

24. Anna Lindberg, 'Transformation of Marriage Patterns in the Kerala Diaspora in the US,' in Knut A. Jacobsen and Pratap Kumar (eds), 2004, *South Asians in the Diaspora: Histories and Religious Traditions*, Leiden: Brill, 203–19, 206.
25. Amitabh Kundu, 2009 (June), 'Urbanisation and Migration: An Analysis of Trends, Patterns and Policies in Asia,' UNDP (Human Development Reports) Research Paper, 1–59, 4–6.
26. Lessinger in Parekh et al., op. cit., 169.
27. Ibid., 171.
28. Anand Giridharadas, 2011, *India Calling: An Intimate Portrait of a Nation's Remaking*, New York: Henry Holt and Company, 2.
29. Grabowski and Grabowski, 190.
30. Ibid., 190–91.
31. Ibid., 193.
32. See David D. Van Tassel and John J. Grabowski, 1987 and 1996, *The Encyclopedia of Cleveland History*, Bloomington: Indian University Press.
33. *Cleveland Ethnic Directory*, 1990, Nationalities Services Center: Cleveland, xxi. {permission to quote information was granted by Dr John Grabowski (on the Advisory Committee for the Ethnic Directory)}
34. Anna Lindberg, 'Transformation of Marriage Patterns in the Kerala Diaspora in the US,' in Knut A. Jacobsen and Pratap Kumar (eds), 2004, *South Asians in the Diaspora: Histories and Religious Traditions*, Leiden: Brill, 203–219, 206.
35. Personal communication with Paramjit Singh, Cleveland, (February and April 2010)
36. Martin Raumann, 2004, 'Becoming a Colour of the Rainbow: Social Integration of Indian Hindus in Trinidad, Analysed Along a Phase Model of Diaspora,' in Knut A. Jacobsen and P. Pratap Kumar (eds), *South Asians in the Diaspora: Histories and Religious Traditions*, Leiden: Brill, 77–96, 79.
37. Cynthia J. Miller, 2008,'Immigrants, Images and Identity: Visualising Homelands Across Borders,' in Parvati Raghuram, Ajaya Kumar Sahoo et al. (eds), *Tracing an Indian Diaspora: Contexts, Memories and Representations*, New Delhi: Sage, 284–98, 284.

38. Miller, 287.
39. Nathan Glazer and Patrick Moynihan, 1963, *Beyond the Melting Pot: the Negroes, Puerto Ricans, Jews, Italians, and Irish of New York City*, Cambridge, MA: MIT Press.
40. Martin Sökefeld, 2000, 'Religion or culture? Concepts of identity in the Alevi diaspora,' Paper presented at a Conference on Locality, Identity, Diaspora, University of Hamburg, 23.

CHAPTER 3

Breaking the Silence

Nostalgia and Memories

With education as the main inspiration, some of the first Indians who came to Ohio and have settled in Cleveland since 1960, have left an indelible mark on the successful trajectories that account for their braving all odds in a foreign land at a very young age. This section is specifically written to honor them for the place they made for themselves and the contributions they have made to the American social and cultural diversity; it is about the dynamics of their loyalty to their Indian cultural past in the process of adaptation and adoption of new cultural values. While it would have been a privilege to include them all, given the time constraints and practical issues in approaching and contacting all of them, this was, regrettably impossible. However, I hope I have done justice by providing a platform for further studies that will provide newer insights into the successful paths of some of the first Asian Indians not only in Cleveland, Ohio, but also in other regions in America.

The following narratives, written *verbatim*, are a presentation of the past experiences, based on shared memories and nostalgia of some of the first Asian Indians who came to Cleveland to adopt it as their new home. Needless to say, these are more than a personal recollection of their past. For they also show how memories of personal experiences tend to fuse personal biography with cultural history.[1] In addition, discourses on memory display a variety of interpretations on the actual meaning and significance of memories in an individual's life. Sometimes, construed as nostalgic, they are seen

> as a complex way in which people bring together past and present lives.[2]

Imbued with nostalgic sentiments, through these experiences they have been able to break the lingering silence coming out of oblivion and anonymity. I was fortunate to be part of personal communications and interactions with all of them (as discussed in this study) in Cleveland. Their personal memories of initial dislocation and the willingness with which these were shared with me, have meant a lot for this study. Promoted by personal images, these also revealed memories and cultural encounters that they had held unvoiced and 'silent' for several decades and I hope I have done justice to their worth by rendering their memories and images indispensable through this study. The study is based on some of the early Asian Indians that came to Northeast Ohio. These include Dr Ashok Pradhan, Ajeet Singh Sood, Sham Gautam, Dr Farookh Screwvala and Paramjit Singh (mentioned in the order of the year of their arrival in Cleveland). Most women who came to Cleveland at the time accompanied their husbands, while very few chose to emigrate alone and independently to foreign nations at the time. Dr Minal Pradhan and Dr Kamala Nagpaul, coming from an affluent educated background in India, accompanied their husbands and adopted Cleveland as their second home after marriage. So did Dr Gita Gidwani who came from Bombay (now Mumbai), and settled in Cleveland with her husband and family. It is with kind permission of all the respondents that the names mentioned in this chapter are actual.

An important feature that characterizes the Indian diaspora is its collective imagining of India emotions, links, traditions, feelings and attachments that together continue to nourish a psychological appeal among successive generations of emigrants from the 'mother' country.[3]

From these new imaginings, emerge new sites within which new social organizations and ethnic mobilizations are visualized. The engagements of individual case studies and their experiences discussed in the following pages are indicative of such mobilizations and the dynamics of their social and cultural relations within a new culture. In understanding their trajectory, notions of 'self' and 'belonging' are visible through their individual experiences.

Dr Ashok Pradhan hails from a family of Barristers-at-Law in Bombay (now Mumbai). His father, Dr Vinayak Pradhan, was a physician, trained in Bombay and London. During World War II, he volunteered to serve in the British Army and was commissioned as a Colonel; he later served as Chief of Karachi American Military Hospital where he took charge of the casualties from General McArthur's campaigns in Burma and the Far East but faced an untimely death in 1948 while treating patients in a typhoid epidemic in Bombay. Dr Ashok Pradhan's mother, Sarojini, was born in an aristrocratic family of Kathewad Diwanji (Premier of Kathewad) – a title bestowed on her great grandfather (the then Chief of the Army) by the Maharaja of the Maratha empire. Throughout her life, Sarojini remained active in several humanitarian services and in 1998 was felicitated at the International Women's Day in Bombay for her lifelong work for women's causes and her services to the community and her country. She died at the age of ninety-eight in December 2008.

Plate 5

Dr Ashok and Dr Minal Pradhan (Dr Ashok Pradhan came to Cleveland in 1959 and Dr Minal Pradhan came in 1962)

Dr Pradhan's career and trajectory is a clear reflection of the manner in which immigrants construct new social relations as part of reaffirming the sense of belonging while trying to forge new identities in a new and distinct culture. On this note, my interactions with Dr Pradhan revealed memories that were also imbued with emotions, attachment and connection with their homeland, India, which reifies their relationship because

> as place combines experience and memory, so, together, do they imbue place.[4]

Recently, Dr Ashok Pradhan celebrated fifty years of his residence in Cleveland, happily recalling his early years of experience prior to and during his residence here.[5] He started his Doctorate degree in 1957 in Jet and Rocket Propulsion at the Imperial College in London. With an immediate urgency to meet the technological need for space activities at the time and by invitation from the then Case Institute of Technology, Dr Pradhan got an opportunity to work as a Research Fellow.

Upon his arrival in Cleveland, he was welcomed by the then Director of Cleveland Council of World Affairs (CCWA) – an organization that also operated an International Students Group (ISG), with meetings on Friday evenings for American and international students to get together socially. This also gave him an opportunity to meet his host families with whom Dr Pradhan cherishes his friendship till date. It is clear that the new social relations from his interactions with professionals at his place of work and educational institutions, created social bonds which facilitated his mobility within the new culture. His experiences also reverberate acceptance from the host community – a factor largely responsible for enabling a successful creation of new identities in a new social space.

Besides, Dr Pradhan also recalled his productive association with NASA in its support for pursuing higher academic interests under the sponsorship of major companies; in particular, the Pneumo-Dynamics Corporation on the Development of Auxiliary Power Systems, and Borg Warner Corporation on Zero-Gravity Vapor Liquid Separators. And with professional success came Dr Pradhan's ability to carve out successful trajectories which went a long way in maintaining cultural continuity with change in his new home in Cleveland. Over the years, both Dr Pradhan and his wife have maintained a large circle of friends which they value and cherish with dignity till date, valuing them as 'role models for their children and grandchildren,' remarked Dr Pradhan. Describing himself as a 'party man,' Dr Pradhan keeps his interests animated through membership to one X-Y Society which has political satire as one of the agendas, besides holding regular sport activities namely, golf, tennis, badminton, racket ball, health clubs, swimming, ice skating, chess, and bridge. Recently, Dr Ashok and Dr Minal Pradhan celebrated fifty years of their residence in Cleveland, which was also an expression of their gratitude to fellow friends and mentors who facilitated their stay in Cleveland over the years.

An important change in the process of migration has been the role of women migrants. They have also formed a large proportion of migrant professionals, including those in the medical profession. Arguably, thus, transmigrant women, after marriage, have played an important role in building and maintaining social relations.[6] Bearing these significant conceptualisations in mind, it is imperative to draw upon women migrants as being indispensable to our understanding of the diasporic dynamics. While the inclusion of a few women in this study is by no means exhaustive, it is equally significant and is also in line with my eventual aim to inspire more detailed works in future, to understand women's role and contributions in shaping the Asian Indian trajectory in Northeast Ohio.

Dr Ashok Pradhan's wife, Dr Minal Pradhan, was born and raised in Bombay and graduated in medicine from the University of Bombay. Minal studied medicine so she could look after a maternity hospital owned by her uncle, Dr S.N. Bhansali. Later, her work experience with Dr V.N. Shirodkar,[8] fetched her a job, more readily than she had envisaged, when she came to Cleveland in 1962. After completing her Fellowship, she chose to work part-time with the Family Planning Center in Cleveland so she could raise her two sons.

In understanding Dr Minal Pradhan's career path as a woman professional in Cleveland, issues of gender and gender discrimination come to the fore. In those days, when foreign medical women were far and few, she recalled issues in getting patients as a practicing physician. American women patients preferred male physicians to women doctors for consultations. A long and difficult trajectory under these circumstances, Dr Minal Pradhan's experiences portray her varied achievements, such as a Fellowship at the University Hospitals in Obstetrics Anaesthesia, and later as an Anaesthesiologist on the staff of Mt. Sinai Hospital for two years, before joining Kaiser Permanente in 1972. Despite the barriers, she not only founded the Anesthesia Department at the Kaiser Hospital in Cleveland but also occupied the Chair of the Department for a few years.

Sham Gautam (Plate 6) came to United States in 1954, with the aim of studying for a professional degree. He spent two years in California before joining the University of Colorado in 1956, where he graduated in Chemical Engineering in 1958. After his marriage in 1959, in Denver, Colorado, Sham Gautam moved to Cleveland for a job. Since there were only a handful of Indians at the time, the chances of socializing with them were almost remote. It was not until early 1960s when, with the prospering engineering and industrial opportunities, more immigrants from India had started coming to Cleveland. His initial years in Cleveland, Sham Gautam recalls, proved very difficult and isolating. In 1962, Sham met V.K. Krishna Menon[9] (Plate 7) who had come to Cleveland to participate in the death anniversary of a railroad magnet in Cleveland.

Plate 6

Sham Gautam (came to Cleveland in 1959)

Plate 7

Sham Gautam and others with V.K. Krishna Menon

In 1963, Sham Gautam met Shanti Bahadur in downtown Cleveland. Shanti Bahadur, in his 70s at the time, was apparently, the oldest Indian in the State of Ohio, who had made a good living with a photography shop he owned in Cleveland. Sham Gautam remained with him until his death, following a long period of ill health, in 1990. With the influx of Indians in later years, cultural connections with India and mobility became feasible, much to the relief of the few Indians in Cleveland. In mid-1970s, Vijay Lakshmi Pandit[10] made an official visit to Case Western Reserve University. Reminiscing the event, Sham Gautam recalls taking Shanti Bahadur to the function. 'As we entered the hall,' said Sham Gautam, 'Vijay Lakshmi Pandit saw Shanti Bahadur, got off the podium and greeted us publicly in the middle of the hall. Shanti Bahadur introduced me to Mrs Pandit and told her that I had adopted him as my elder to take care of him in his old age.' In the second half of 1960s, Sham Gautam felt more settled in as he slowly involved himself in the Indian social and cultural events in Cleveland. He recalls,

> 'I became a citizen of United States in 1965. And by 1967, I registered the first Sikh Temple in Cleveland because no Sikh at that time was a US citizen. When we bought the FICA building in Cleveland Heights, all merchants were against it, for they feared that it would affect their business. At that point, my friends persuaded me to help them tide over issues emerging from this. I contacted a few businessmen who had stores in the neighborhood. On the day of the hearing at the City Hall to discuss the issue of having FICA office in Cleveland, about six FICA members, including myself, accompanied by a few businessmen went to the meeting. The Director read the charter and FICA application then asked for the vote. Fortunately, FICA application was approved by the majority. In 1978, I served FICA as its President serving until my retirement in 1997 from Ford Motor Company. I am enjoying my retirement now.'[11]

Cultural connections with India reinforced the much needed trajectories that strengthened individual ties and identities. As visibly marked in the late 1960s and 70s, they found expression through various social events, using radio and films as the connecting link, thus reaffirming cultural links with their counterparts in India (Plate 8).

In addition, the film industry, which has always been the biggest source of entertainment in India, remained popular amongst the few Asian Indians in Cleveland. Cultural representations in these forms from homeland, Miller remarks,

> serve as resources for the construction of a new sort of knowledge-endangering new relationships ... that anchor

Plate 8

Connecting with India through Indian music via the local radio

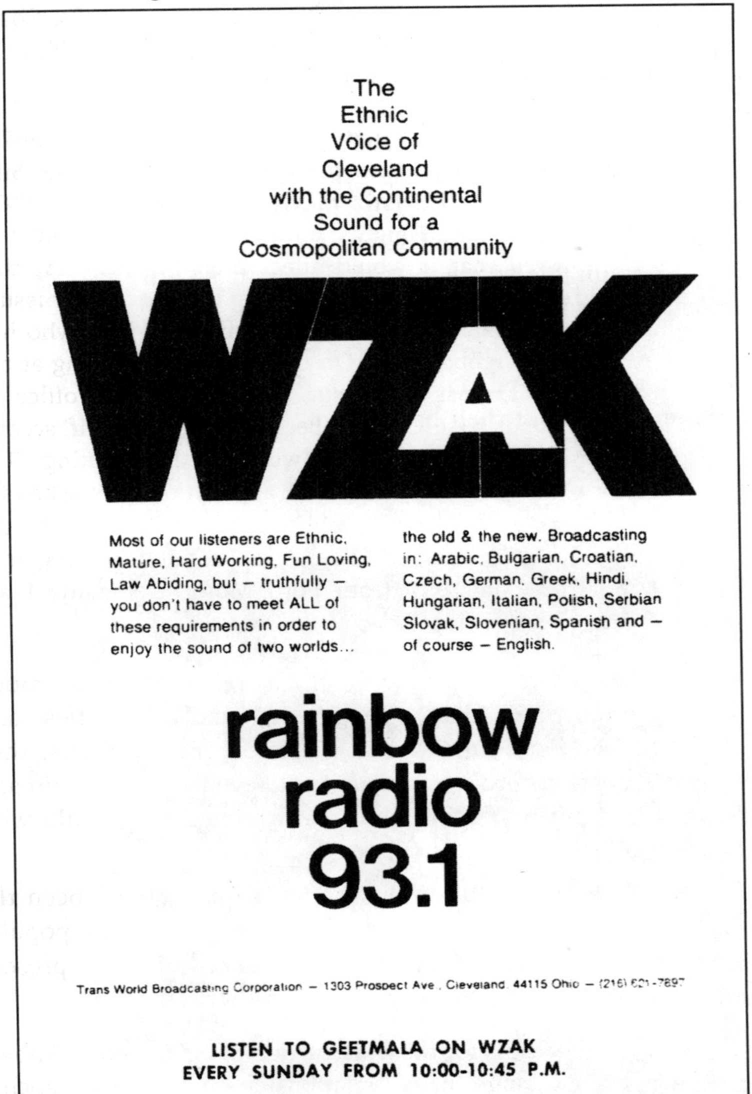

immigrants' identities and creating a mental template for memories of home.[12]

In the early years of the 1970s, radio and films provided the major source of entertainment not only in India but also in Cleveland for the Asian Indians. In Ohio, it remained a popular source of entertainment, especially at a time when culture and linguistic links with India were difficult to establish initially. Occasionally, lead singers of the film industry (Plate 9) were invited to perform at various musical and social events which provided a suitable venue for social meetings with members of the Asian Indian community.

My own interaction and personal interviews with some of the first group of Asian Indians in Cleveland revealed shared common facts about their background – firstly, most Sikhs who

Plate 9

Mohammad Rafi (the late lead singer of Indian film industry) invited to perform in Cleveland (seen here with Sham Gautam)

came to Cleveland belonged to a highly skilled group of engineers from the northern part of India, Punjab, and secondly, their association with the American engineering firms, who were in India to oversee the construction of some of the major water dams in Punjab, made them more amenable to new opportunities for work in the US at the behest of these firm managers. Thus, going back to the early and late 1960s, a majority of Asian Indians who came and settled in Cleveland were skilled professionals, especially, engineers who were successful in seeking prestigious jobs in Cleveland. These include Joginder S. Dhillon, RanjitSingh, Harbans Sandhu, Paramjit Singh, Ajeet Singh Sood, Pritam S. Bhatia and Harmehan S. Sethi. Except for Paramjit Singh and Ajeet Singh Sood, the others chose not to stay behind, and as such it was feasible to retrieve any information about them; together, they were seen as a 'Colony.' (Plate 10)

While the acceptance and assimilation of new culture remained paramount in the ideologies of the Asian Indian community, significant markers in this direction facilitated these efforts. For instance, the formation in October 1964 of The India Association of Cleveland (Plate 11. For details on the Constitution, see Appendix) provided an inspiration

> to share and present the rich cultural tradition and customs to American friends and to provide opportunities for cultural exchange and encourage close ties amongst Indians in Cleveland, which often found expression in sharing celebrations of various Indian festivals and national holidays.[13]

At the same time, new and favourable modifications in the Constitution of the India Association of Cleveland, led to the establishment of an India House to serve the Indian community in Cleveland. This also marked renewed interest in the political issues at the time (Plate 12), for it represented establishing contacts through institutions and networks. While institutional changes helped strengthen close ties, the Asian Indian

Plate 10

'Colony' of Sikhs in Cleveland (courtesy of Ajeet Singh Sood, from his personal collection, communication October 2010) (L to R: Jasjeet Singh Sood (8) and Joginder S. Dhillon (first row); Ranjit Singh and Harbans S. Sandhu (second row); Paramjit Singh and Ajeet S. Sood (third row); Pritam S. Bhatia and Harmehan S. Sethi (back row)

Plate 11

The India Association of Cleveland and its Constitution

India
association of
Cleveland
For the Advancement of the Indian Community

CONSTITUTION

(This Constitution was adopted and ratified in April 1964, and amended in December 1968, August 1969, February 1972, October 1972 and September 1973).

ARTICLE I Name and Objectives

Section 1 The name of the Association shall be India Association of Cleveland.

Section 2 The objectives of the Association shall be to educate, promote and present a clear picture of Indian traditions, customs and recent Indian developments to the people of Cleveland, Ohio; arrange for the celebration of Indian national holidays, foster closer ties among the Indians in Cleveland, Ohio, and to promote friendship and cultural exchange with other Associations, organizations and groups, foreign and American, in Ohio.

ARTICLE II Membership

Section 1 Membership in the Association shall be of three classes:

a) Regular Members
b) Associate Members
c) Honorary Members

Section 2 a) Regular Members: These shall be any Indian citizens over the age of 16 who are interested in the objectives of the Association.

b) Associate Members: These shall be non-Indians above the age of 16 who are interested in the objectives of the Association.

c) Honorary Members: These shall be nominated by the Executive Board of the Association. Such members are not required to be Indian citizens.

Section 3 Annual dues shall be: $4.00 per year for single members; $6.00 per year for married couples. No dues shall be required of Honorary Members. (As amended in September 1973)

ARTICLE III Officers of Executive Board

Section 1 The Officers of the Association shall be a President, Vice President, Treasurer, Secretary, Joint Secretary and four Committee members, all of whom shall comprise the Executive Board of nine.

Section 2 The Officers shall be elected once a year at the Annual Meeting of the Association Membership which shall be held in the month of February.

Section 3 No member shall be eligible to contest for election to the same office for more than two times consecutively.

Section 4 The President shall be an ex officio member of all committees.

Plate 12

Indians and the emerging political engagements

IAC GENERAL BODY MEETING ON FEBRUARY 17

India Association of Cleveland will hold its annual general body meeting on Sunday, February 17, 1974, at 2:00 p.m. in the Schmitt Auditorium of Case Western Reserve University. This announcement should be treated by the members as the notice of the meeting.

ANNUAL ELECTIONS

According to Article III (Section 2) of the Constitution enclosed, the elections of the IAC will also be held at the same time on February 17. The "Regular Members" of IAC desiring to contest the election for the nine positions in the executive committee and one auditor should send in their nominations by mail so as to reach on or before **Friday, January 25, 1974**, to the following address:

L. N. Sampath, President
India Association of Cleveland
4709½ Walford Road, Apt. 10
Warrensville Heights, Ohio 44128

Nominations should include the nominee's name, address, telephone number and signature. Nominees should be dues paid members of IAC for the year 1974. They must also be Indian citizens as required by the Association's Constitution. Nominations can be withdrawn on or before **Monday, January 28, 1974**, by mail or telephone by calling L. N. Sampath at 831-9373.

Cont'd...

...Cont'd

BOARD OF GOVERNORS OF INDIA HOUSE PROJECT

As reported in THE LOTUS last month, the following members have been appointed to the Board of Governors of the India House Project:

Kanti Patel for 1973-76
Paramjit Singh for 1973-76
Sukumar Roy for 1973-75
B. K. Srinivas for 1973-75

The above members of the Board of Governors are subject to confirmation by the General Body in the February meeting. Nominations for two more members of the Board of Governors for the period 1974-77 are invited from the membership. The nominations with name, address, telephone number and signature may be sent to Mr. L. N. Sampath at the address indicated above before Friday, January 25. Nominations can be withdrawn before Monday, January 28. Any dues-paid member of IAC can send in his or her nomination for the Board of Governors. The election will be held along with the election of officers of IAC.

CONSTITUTIONAL AMENDMENTS

The updated Constitution of IAC is enclosed in this issue of THE LOTUS. According to Article XI of the Constitution, the by-laws may be modified or amended by majority vote of the membership, if prior notice is mailed to members two weeks in advance of the meeting.

If you want to send in your proposal for constitutional amendment, please send it by mail so as to reach on or before Friday, January 25, 1974, to the following address:

India Association of Cleveland
Post Office Box No. 5206
Cleveland, Ohio 44101
Attention: Narendra Chawla, Secretary

The constitutional amendment proposals can be withdrawn on or before Monday, January 28, 1974, by mail or telephone by calling Narendra Chawla at 248-8329.

The names of the nominees along with the details of the general body meeting will appear in the February issue of THE LOTUS.

community made constant efforts in taking Asian Indian culture to residents of Cleveland. Its members held congregations where they explained and demonstrated the philosophy of Indian religions, for instance Sikhism, which has existed as one of the great religions of India. While this was part of creating awareness about global religions, it also enabled them to maintain religious ties with the country they left. Emphasis on highlighting the diversity indicated that religious traditions and their rituals and practices could be learnt not only from scriptures and religious texts, but also from communications and practical demonstrations in the public sphere. These were either done at special gatherings or events in Cleveland. The presence and participation of other communities at such events also meant the creation of mutual perceptions of cultures and how they influenced daily lives within a local space. Additionally, funds were raised by the Sikh community to establish a Sikh temple which created newer social and religious alliances amongst the people as well as provided a suitable venue for social gatherings.

The early years of settlement in the new land also called for promoting cultural aspects of India in Cleveland. Sikhs, as representing the majority of Indians in Cleveland at the time, remained enthusiastic about enriching an understanding of diversity at the popular level, at the same time accommodating new cultural mores. Regular *dewans* were held to inform the people about Sikh culture and customs[14] (Plate 13) as also important elements, teachings and history. Besides, various social events were held to collect funds to support similar social and cultural events which would reach as well as facilitate integration of Asian Indian culture within the local Cleveland community (Plate 14).

Like his contemporaries, Ajeet Singh Sood also came to Cleveland in the year 1960 (Plate 15). Hailing from Punjab, in the north-western part of India, Ajeet Sood worked in the Punjab

Plate 13

Invitation to attend Sikh 'Dewan' in Cleveland (courtesy of Ajeet Singh Sood, from his personal collection, communication October 2010)

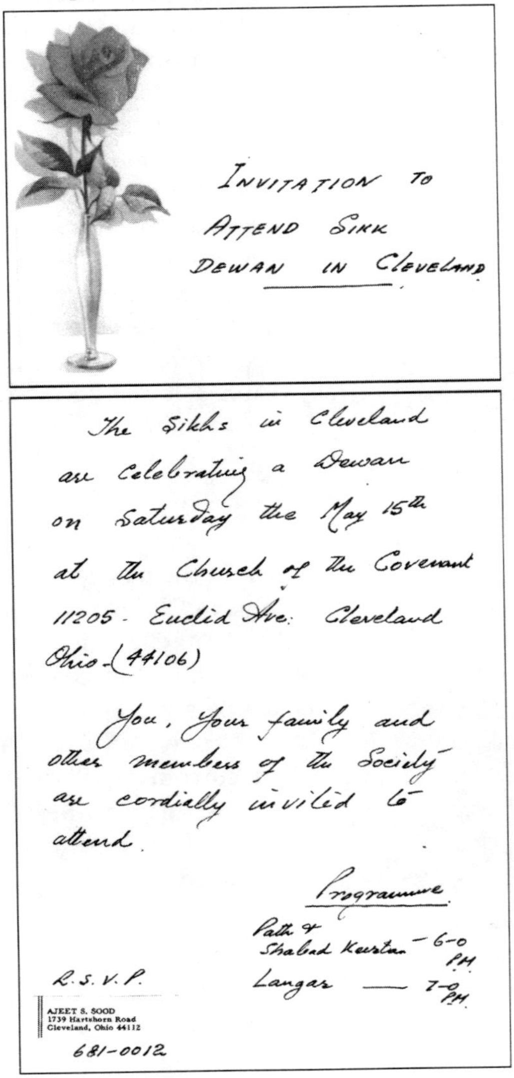

INVITATION TO
ATTEND SIKK
DEWAN IN CLEVELAND

The Sikhs in Cleveland
are Celebrating a Dewan
on Saturday the May 15th
at the Church of the Covenant
11205 - Euclid Ave. Cleveland
Ohio - (44106)

You, Your family and
other members of the Society
are cordially invited to
attend.

Programme.

Path &
Shabad Keertan — 6-0 P.M.
Langar — 7-0 P.M.

R.S.V.P.

AJEET S. SOOD
1739 Hartshorn Road
Cleveland, Ohio 44112

681-0012

Public Works department as an Assistant Design Engineer, working with US specialization on the design and construction of various elements of the Bhakra Dam, one of the world's largest gravity structures. He held several prestigious positions not only in Cleveland, but also in Atlanta, Washington and Virginia.

Plate 14

Funds for Sikh Temple (personal communication, courtesy of Ajeet Singh Sood from his personal collection, communication October 2010)

A SALE FOR SIKHS — Mrs. Noor Durry, a member of the Sikh Cultural Society, displays some of the handcrafts that will be sold to help the Sikhs raise money for a temple in the southeast suburbs. To help raise funds, the society is sponsoring "Glimpses of the Cultural Heritage of India," at 8 p.m. Saturday in Bedford High School, 475 Northfield Rd. Admission is $2.50 per person. In addition to the handicrafts, there will be dances, music and a fashion show. (Press photo by Fred Bottomer)

Plate 15

Ajeet Singh Sood (came to Cleveland in 1960) and wife, Joginder Sood (came to Cleveland in 1961)

Ajeet Singh Sood narrates a long and engaging history of his personal experiences imbued with varied memories. Here is a revelation into the early years of Ajeet Singh Sood in Cleveland, as we go back into his personal experiences as the first turbaned Sikh who came to Cleveland, Ohio (and now lives in Maryland), followed by his student days at the Case Institute of Technology (as it was then called).

> I was a young Sikh from Punjab state India, serving the Indian Government as an Assistant Design Engineer on the design of Bhakra Dam and ventured to come to the States for higher studies. Having worked with the Dam Design Team (Technical Cooperative Mission) for eight years, I took a firm decision to come to the US in 1960, leaving my wife and two children – boy (2 years) and girl (8 months). I left Bombay via an Italian ship, *Lauro Folota,* on August 29th 1960, which was the

cheapest way to reach Europe in 17 days. Disembarking the ship in Naples, I railed to England from where Pan Am brought me to JFK Airport in New York (14 September 1960) where I was received by a friend, Mr W, a TCM consultant UNO employee, who I knew from Delhi. Mr W drove me to his office in New York, and introduced me as 'a turbaned friend from India' to all his colleagues, treated me to lunch, and finally put me on Grey Hound Bus to Cleveland. A tired, different looking Indian with a turban became a focal point for everyone to stare at. It would have been a long and boring bus journey, but a person sitting next to me asked if I spoke English. A little later, he took out a chess board from bag and asked if I could play with him. This broke the monotony and the whole night was spent in the bus playing chess. Finally, in the early hours of 15 September 1960, the driver announced arrival in Cleveland. It was the start of a new life. The Department of Foreign Students' Advisers of Case Institute of Technology, the then boys' school in Advanced Engineering and Research, had made the necessary arrangements for welcoming foreign students. Following a reception, each one was assigned a host family which they called 'a home away from home.' I joined Atalas's family in Shaker Heights, Ohio. Gene and Sanford Atalas with two children were a great help to get me set and achieve goals for which I came. This system provided a great moral support for all those who were strangers in a foreign land, but for me it was more so because of my appearance. This was the beginning of strange experiences of life in America. Besides, burdened by tough school work, after an eight-year gap from school, I recall several experiences, some interesting and others reflecting upon my identity.

It was not only the dress and the appearance but also my accent and pronunciation of certain words such as Alumenium (instead of Aluminum), and calling columns as stanchions, etc. which caused some embarrassment during my first class presentation. Students like me, who ran out of funds, started job hunting. On the one hand, I was lucky to have experience in India of working with the cream of American engineers but on the other hand, I was different looking which made life more challenging and interesting.[15]

Ajeet Singh Sood created a new chapter in Cleveland history, by being the first turbaned Sikh to graduate from the (then) Case Institute of Technology in June 1963, (although he successfully completed his degree in December 1962 – Plate 16) and in 1972, he completed his business degree (MBA) from Case Western Reserve University.

With this recognition, the gradual social and cultural acceptance of the diverse groups became apparent. Needless to say, the efforts of the first Indians who came to Cleveland in the 1960s did not go unheeded and proved indispensable to the new cultural diversity in Cleveland at the time. In some high schools, small events were held to mark the International Day, thus signifying the growing plural culture (Plate 17). By the 1970s, Asian Indians in Northeast Ohio were gradually involving themselves in local social events. The presence of cultural groups for people who hailed from different regions of India, as in Bengal, Tamil Nadu, Gujarat, comprised the Federation of India Community Associations which operated from a community centre in Cleveland Heights.

In the meanwhile, other social events engaging the Asian Indian community in Cleveland continued to make the city more culturally vibrant. The singles' club called the Youth India Club, brought together young men and women, and a nationwide activity, Project India, was founded under the aegis of the Associations of Indians in America of New York.[16] Besides, the India House Project raised funds to support classes for children to learn Indian dance, music and languages.[17] There were deliberate attempts to encourage the Asian Indians to retain their connections with their homeland for which modest air fares were offered to facilitate links with India (Plate 18).

Plate 16

Ajeet Singh Sood at the graduation ceremony at the (then) Case Institute of Technology in Cleveland

PAGE E 6

Turbaned Grad Waits Case Diploma

By BUD WEIDENTHAL

Four hundred seventy-six scientists and engineers, garbed in cap and gown, will receive their diplomas from Case Tech at commencement exercises tomorrow.

One other will wear turban and gown.

The precedent breaker is A. S. Sood, an Indian, and a member of the Sikh religion. Sikhs must wear the turban as part of their dress at all times.

No Mortarboard

It is the first time in the memory of veteran Case officials that a graduate will walk in the ceremonial procession without wearing the traditional mortarboard.

This caused a minor stir among Case administrators. But, says Sood: "They were very kind about it and suggested I appear at graduation in full national dress. But I have decided that would be too conspicuous."

Sood will receive his master of science degree in engineering mechanics. He is employed as a stress analyst at the Hoff Research and Development laboratory in East Cleveland.

E. Cleveland Resident

Sood and his family—he is married and has two small children — arrived in Cleveland in September, 1960. They live at 1739 Hartshorne Rd., East Cleveland.

Tomorrow's commencement at Severance Hall will be a precedent breaker in other ways. It will be the first time that Case will award a master's degree in the history of technology. In addition, more doctor's degrees—a total of 52—will be awarded than in any previous year.

Speaker at the commencement exercises will be Dr. Marcel Roche, director of the Venezuelan Institute for Scientific investigation.

Here is the list of the degree candidates:

TURBAN AND GOWN will be the graduation garb of A. S. Sood when he receives his master's degree from Case Tech tomorrow.

Bachelor of Science

Astronomy

Edward Coyne, William Kovach, Theodore Simon, Chris Terrill

Chemistry

William Baizer, John Bdzil Jr., Dennis Davis, Kirk Davis, Richard Demchak, Adam Dreisziger, Duane Heyman, Walter Kelly, Fred Kohl, Frank Mendicino, William Nebe, James Oziomek, John Petz, Melvin Pleiss Jr., Theodore Rapp, David Roice, Joseph Wander, [illegible] Wilczynski

Chemical Engineering

William Cares, Yu Chi Go Co, William Eberhardt, Melvin Ehrlich, William Faith, William Hendricks Jr., William Jenkins, William Jones, Tibor Kis, Carl Koch, Phillip Krasen, Alfredo Nogueria, Gabriel Ortega, Todd Pitts, Gary Szitas, John Thayer

Civil Engineering

Victor Carter, Lawrence Cox, Jack Fleming, Richard Grum, Arvind Joshi, William La Pay, Christopher Mathewson, Richard Peruzzini, Harold Pohler, Donald Rauch, Frank Razinger, David Rocovits, Edmund Rybicki, Thomas Uiterdyke

Electrical Engineering

Louis Aliberti, David Allborn, Robert Barnett, Robert Burhanna, Nicholas Camino, William Cap, Robert Carr, Richard Cassel, Thomas Cleaver, Jerry Condren, Dennis Corsello, Kenneth Daggs, William Delly, Richard Dibbs, Stephen Dobler, Philip Eberhart, David Falcon, Paul Friday, Thomas Kraynak, Dale La Plante, Chinh Le, Robert Lenz, Kenneth Leonhardt, Ark Lew, Thomas Laike, Gerald Mook, James Moorhead, Fred Mullen, Albin Muren, Lee Owen, Raymond Paciorek, Raymond Pyles, John Rasmussen, James Rybak, John Sala, Thomas Scoccia, James Glover, James Grau, William Gromen, Larry Hennessee, Dan Hilberman, Ernest Hofmeister, Bernard Huth, Victor Ilenda, Aleksander Karcic, David Kaus, Edward Ketterlingham, Robert Kihm, John Skok, Leslie Smith, James Snediker, John Spisak, Donald Squires, Charles Steffey, Frederick Stevenson Jr., John Thomas, Paul Vargo Jr., Richard Vidmar, Kermit Wall, Joseph Wotowiec

Engineering Science

David Alexander, Mark Asadow, Gerald Barna, Paul Bondor, Richard Buta, Patrick Carney, James Harrass, Carl Helrich Jr., William Johnson, Robert Kern, Paul King, Richard Kurrle, Edward Maroll, Dennis Millett, Gerald Petac, Richard Prutow, Harry Raber, Richard Robrock II, James Sadowski, John Sato, James Scott, Frank Stilwagner, Robert Udell, Richard Weber, David Withrow

Mechanical Engineering

John Barni, Harry Begg, Thomas Bergin, Jon Beyer, Raymond Bilski, Erling Bjornrud, Bruce Bretschneider, James Burda, Edward Corell, Allen Curl, Kishore Dalal, George Duleba, Robert Follett, Louis Goldish, Larry Gordon, Robert Grguric, John Haessly, Donald Hale, Erik Halvorsen, Rodolfo Hollander, Joseph Jacobs, Harry Keller Jr., Sheldon Kovit, Waldemar Krewedl, Charles Lavan Jr., Barry Licht, Frank Linsalata, Roy Lottig, Carlos Ivo da Costa Mendes, Ronald Meszoros, Thomas Militano, Harvey Nathanson, David Nethery, Jeffrey Noss, David Ridenour, William Sandy Jr., John Scotchie, John Shadley, David Siembieda, Lawrence Simon, Richard Strancar, Joseph Thompson, Robert Vukosic, David Wilson, John Zawada

Management Science

Mahabir Agarwal, Gary Barr, Lewis Beals, Paul Begany, Roger Cerne, Henry Clark Jr., Robert Cooke, Daniel Coviello, Martin Geisel, Peter Hanley, David Hunt, Michael Jacobs, Larry Kaufer, William Kieffer, Dale Kincaid, John Kluber, Roy Larson, Terry Laug, Roger Lourens, Martin Matthews, John McWhorter III, Karl Newkirk, Douglas Pease, Bruce Raimy, Howard Robinson, Laurence Saslaw, Thomas Shepherd, John Sifonis, Gary Silverman, David Simon, Sammy Snyder, Terry Troy, Bruce Werstak

Mathematics

George Baumanis, John Bergin, Gerald Dankner, Norman Fischer, Donald Golden, Lawrence Horwitz, William Johnson, Russell Mayers, Kendall Pim, Robert Schweitz, Stephen Sedlak, Jeffrey Stone, Kenneth Walter

Metallurgical Engineering

Dennis Bench, Charles Bowman, David DeSante, Martin Faigus, Robert Fedor, Stanley Gluck, George Good, David Haley, Jacob Haser, Igor Komarjanski, Frank Krotine, Jon McGraw, John McGreer, Edward Morgan Jr., Dennis Paulin, Laszlo Sandor, Dominic Strollo, Valdis Svekis, Dandridge Tomalin, Dominic Toriello, Richard Vybnal, Clarence Weidner Jr., Robert Wight

Physics

Eugene Aughinbaugh, John Axline, David Bebko, Ronald Bousek, Charles Boyer, Vince Cermak, Thomas Derkacs, Barry Fell, Porter Johnson, William King, Kenneth Koral, James Lindow, Carroll Mannon, Paul Mantsch, Kenneth Millard, David Morgan, William Oran, John Pierce, Thomas Sampson, Eli Sank, Gary Sega, David Seiler, Dennis Skala, Gary Smith, William Spiegelberg, Frederick Strnisa Jr., Jerry Tessin, Donald Weber, Paul Weiss

Master of Science

Thomas Hier, Charles Bolton, Ronald Boyer, Jan Clee, Siska Tine Feenstra, Alan Fitz, Robert Jenks Jr., Lyn Pankoff, James Powers, Melinda Sprague

Chemistry

Carol Haberman

Aeronautical Engineering

John Handley

Chemical Engineering

Kenneth Bowles, Alfonso Perez de Mendoza, James Kousky, Wesley Loos, [illegible]

Mathematics

Frederick Canfield III, William Davis, Robert Fabian, Philip Hip-Chung Fung, Clinton Hoberecht, Richard Kowalski, Melvyn Magree, Frank Molls, Richard Orr, Eleanor Marion Zeitlin Sava, Jonathan Seaman

Metallurgy

John Alexander Jr., Ronald Barto, Nathan Church, Gordon Dobie, Frank Gill, John Kocerha, Carl Nelson, Paul Repas, Joseph Stephens, William Stuhrke

Physics

Gust Bambakidis, Richard Bartels, Frank Blood Jr., Gerald Brown, William Chow, Gale Fair, David Giltinan, Larry Jeffers, James Kurfess, Harold Peters, Robert Plummer, Gerd Schilling, Melvin Shaw, George Spencer, Wayne Sukow, John Tippie, Paul Wolfe

Master of Arts

History of Science and Technology

Marvin Katzman, Charles Weiner

Doctor of Philosophy

William Brunk, Kusumanto Purbosiswolo, Antony Champ, Gordon Cheever, Edward Chenevey, Mu-Tong Chiang, William Kroenke, Paul Kr[illegible], William Strieder, David Vince[illegible], Philip Nachtsheim, Fay Fun, Chi-Chang Lee, Leonard Truesdell Jr., Herbert Weinstein, Eugene Weissman, Walter Workman, Walter Fahey, Altan Ferendeci, Jacob Gustincic, Hari Jethanand Nain, Leonard Stone, Peter Tsivitse, Joseph Gariboldi, Lowell Domholdt, Edwin Kolb, Pau-Chang Lu, Lester Nichols, Erik Trostmann, Teng-chung Wu, Arnold Berger, Noel Mirasol, Jerry Sanders, David Seidman, Eliezer Shlifer, Charles Sprague III, Donald Stewart, Ronald Wolff, William Roodebush, Thomas Herbell, Arthur Kramer, David Laverty, Robert Schafer, William Bassichis, Richard Block, Kenneth Brog, James Corll, Ronald Kaul, James Michael, Roger Miller, Raymond Mountain, Donald Schuele

Plate 17

Celebrating International Day in Cleveland

International Day at Superior

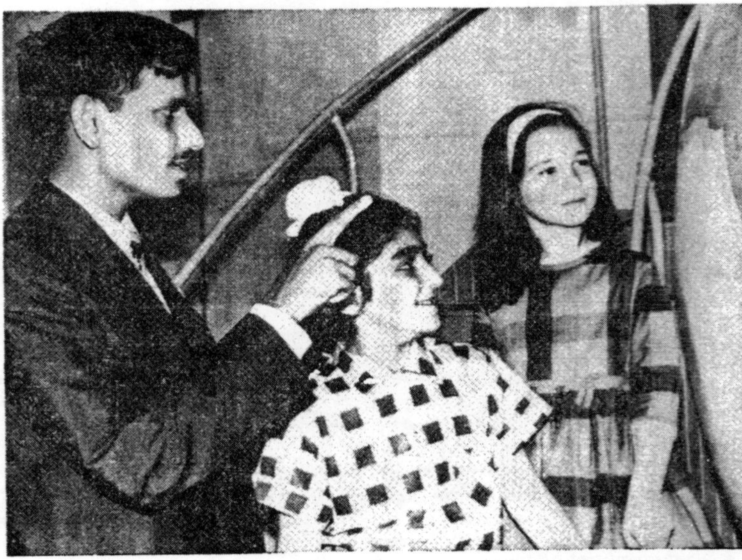

You're a school principal. You have some visitors. You're making introductions.

"Children, I'd like to introduce Miss Sauwalugsna Plooksawasdi and Mrs. Chutatip Pantupongse from Thailand."

PRINICIPAL JANIS Conklin made it the introductions last Friday, as Superior Elementary School had its own International Day.

Miss Plooksawasdi and Mrs. Pantupongse were two of the nine international visitors that added authenticity to the day.

The others who toured the school were Nilkanth Chaudhari of India, Miss Maria Pia Dolci of Italy, Udo Eshiet of Nigeria, Miss Maria Garcia of Uruguay, Miss Ingalill Svensson of Sweden, Miss Paulina Valenzuela of Chile, and Hermann-Josef Voss of Germany.

ALL OF THEM are social or welfare workers in their own countries here on a six-weeks training and orientation tour under the auspices of the Cleveland International Program for Youth Leaders and Social Workers, Inc..

At Superior, they spent the morning watching — first at an auditorium assembly, then in classrooms.

After lunch at Kirk Junior High, they returned to Superior to spend an informal afternoon with the pupils and teachers.

HAPPIEST PART of the day was when the visitors got together with Superior School pupils from their own lands.

In this picture, Nilkanth Claudhari found plenty to talk about with first graders Jasjett Sood (center) and Melani Doodhar, both of Indian descent. They're looking at Superior's second-floor globe.

Plate 18

Links with Indian

Now, on our 14-120 day fare, you can even stop in Delhi and Bombay.

- When you fly to either city, we let you stop over. That's because we're your airline. We know you may have friends and relatives whom you won't want to miss when you return home.
- You can fly with 77 pounds (35 kilos) of free baggage.
- You can stay as few as 14 days or the maximum 120 days. (21 day minimum during June, July, and August.)
- Starting January 9, the roundtrip economy fare is $577, N.Y.-Delhi and/or Bombay, subject to government approval.
- We serve Indian vegetarian or non-vegetarian dishes and Continental cuisine.
- Daily flights from N.Y. to Bombay or Delhi.
- Our music is Indian (classical, light-classical or film features), and Western (we have 4 additional channels).
- Besides music to soothe your ears, we show films to delight your eyes.
- And if you buy tickets here for family and friends in India, you'll save the 10% tax.

At Air-India, we try to bring you home with our Indian warmth and courtesy before you even get there.

Call your travel agent or

AIR-INDIA

666 Fifth Avenue, New York 10019 Tel: (212) 751-6200

We're your airline.

Atlanta (404) 577-2484, Chicago (312) 782-6263, Cleveland (216) 861-2636, Dallas (214) 748-0637, Detroit (313) 963-5500
Los Angeles (213) 624-7071, Mexico City 546-6678, Montreal (514) 866-1213, Philadelphia (215) 563-0480
Port of Spain, Trinidad 35213-35762, San Francisco (415) 362-5746, Toronto (416) 362-6441
Vancouver (604) 681-9226, Washington, D.C. (202) 785-8989

Plate 19

Farookh Screwvala (came to Cleveland in September 1960)

Farookh Screwvala (Plate 19) also came Cleveland in 1960. Born in (the then) Bombay in 1939, he came from a family of industrial magnates who owned several companies, some catering to provisions for hospitals and the navy. Farookh attended Campion School and St. Mary's High School in Mumbai, and after completing the Senior Cambridge School examination, enrolled at St. Xavier's College, completing the first two years towards a Bachelor of Science degree. Thereafter, he entered the Victoria Jubilee Technical Institute to pursue studies in Civil Engineering.

Farookh's journey to the US began more out of peer influence when he decided to follow a close friend, Puran Mehta, to the United States to complete his engineering degree. Together, they applied to the University of Michigan for admission but were unable to get admission as all classes were full. On another friend's recommendation, both requested the University of Michigan to forward their application to the Case Institute of Technology which finally took them to Cleveland. It was a rare privilege, recalls Farookh, to have met the then President, at a special student body meeting in Cleveland. Not only this, the people of Cleveland were very gracious and helpful in welcoming all of the foreign students, making sure that they had good housing and assigned a foster family to each student. Staying with foster families facilitated strong bonds which lasted as lifelong friendships with them.

The sixties were a time when American engineers were in their heyday. They rightly earned the reputation of accomplishing feats that many people thought were impossible. It was a thriving and prosperous time to be an engineering student in Cleveland. The steel mills and other industries were flourishing. Cleveland was full of vibrant, friendly people. There were lots of good restaurants and department stores and plenty of good activities, the Cleveland Orchestra, the Art Museum and the Cleveland Play House. It was a life of work, learning and enjoyment. The Indian student community was small and close knit, and friendships formed then, survive even today.

Farookh Screwvala recalls early days of his association with Case Western Reserve University, after which, in 1964, he went to Northwestern University to study for his doctoral degree. Reflecting upon his graduate days, Farookh Screwvala remarks,

> we worked hard and some of us would go once a week to play bridge at Willmette Women's Club. We were well received by the people who became very good friends but after a while they would be disappointed that more often than not someone from our group would be the winner. In 1967, I

returned to Cleveland to work. I met my wife Ellen and we married in 1968. We have two sons. Our older son, Erach, is a lawyer living in Brooklyn, New York. He has three lovely daughters. Our younger son, Cyrus, lives in Greensburg, Indiana with his wife. He teaches mathematics and physics at the High School. In 1977, I opened my own office and still work from it. Ellen and I have enjoyed living in Bay Village for the last forty five years.

Paramjit Singh (Plate 20), another member of the Asian Indian community, has been a Community Leader of the Asian Indian Community since he landed in Cleveland in June of 1962.

Plate 20

Paramjit Singh and wife Linda Singh

The following account highlights some of the interesting experiences of Paramjit Singh in his own words:

> I completed my Mechanical Engineering from the Indian Institute of Technology (I.I.T.) Kharagpur, India, in 1958 and came to Cleveland in 1962, to work as a trainee for McDowell-Wellman Engineering, while also pursuing a Masters in Business Administration at the then Western Reserve University. As a graduate student, I got involved with the International Student Group and shortly thereafter became its President. This gave me the opportunity to meet students from all over the world, including my wife Linda who was born and raised in Cleveland who I also met during one of the international student events. Coming from India opened up good opportunities to share with my international friends and Clevelanders, the Indian culture, entertainment, food and religions, especially Sikhism (the fifth largest religion in the world). The Cleveland Council of World Affairs asked me to organize the first Indian dinner to celebrate the 13th Republic Day of India with students and members of the Council. In 1964, I got involved with other members of the Indian community to establish the India Association of Cleveland.

Paramjit Singh was yet another Asian Indian who made history in Cleveland by being the first turbaned Sikh to be part of Western Reserve University graduation ceremony, proudly wearing his turban, rather than the traditional mortarboard, in the year 1965 (Plate 21).

With the change in immigration laws and the growth of the Indian community in Cleveland and throughout the United States, the National Federation of Indian-American Association (NFIA) was formed in 1980 and that resulted in the creation of the Federation of India Community Associations of NE Ohio (FICA) in 1981, a member of NFIA. Alongside these major changes in America, some members of the Asian Indian

Plate 21

Paramjit Singh at the graduation ceremony at the (then) Western Reserve

community remained prominent in sharing and reciprocating to the country which provided them with opportunities to establish here. Paramjit Singh and his wife, Linda, thus, were instrumental in creating Project SEVA with Ohio State Senator Michael White and Reverend Earl Preston Jr., Pastor of Morning Star Baptist Church. Project SEVA prepared and served a Thanksgiving Dinner to 400 people at the church. The joy that they experienced, says Paramjit Singh, led him to share it with the Executive Board of NFIA which led to an eventual adoption of Project SEVA as a national project by NFIA.

Paramjit Singh continues to provide his personal and professional time as a volunteer to add value to the Indian and

Ohio community. He has served as President of FICA, Vice President NFIA, President of American Society of Engineers of Indian Origin, Cleveland Chapter, Founding member of Asian-Indian-American Business Group, Asian-Indian-American for Better Government, Executive member of Cleveland Mayor George Voinovich's Asian Advisory Council and more.[18] Most recently, Paramjit Singh, among others, was recognized by The Cleveland International Hall of Fame for his valuable and lasting contribution to Cleveland's multicultural society;[19] the induction ceremony for the inaugural class of the Cleveland International Hall of Fame was held on Wednesday, 12 May 2010, and was attended by over 300 people.

With the increasing opportunities in Cleveland, more Indians came to Cleveland to seek better work opportunities. Dr Gita P. Gidwani came to Cleveland in September 1968. Although she had a comfortable job, social circle, friends and family in Mumbai prior to emigrating to Cleveland in September 1968, she accompanied her husband and family. She had worked at the prestigious Lady Hardinge Medical College in Delhi, India in 1962. Trained in Obstetrics and Gynaecology, she worked at Mumbai's KEM teaching hospital and was quite happily involved raising her family of two children when they uprooted to come to Cleveland. The inspiration to leave India followed her husband's successful travels to Germany and London. As a working mother and a new immigrant, Dr Gidwani could not afford to give any work opportunity a miss and accepted her first job at St. John's hospital on the west side of Cleveland – a job which fulfilled the family requirements of a house as well as a decent remuneration. She got a fully furnished hospital house as part of her house position, and within a week was accepted as a home physician in Obstetrics and Gynaecology.

At a time when only 7 per cent of physicians in the US were women, Dr Gita Gidwani painfully recalls how as a woman, as a foreigner and as a physician, her ordeals never seemed to end – it

Plate 22

Dr Gita P. Gidwani (came to Cleveland in September 1968)

was as though an anomaly in a not so diverse world of Cleveland and she looks back to say,

> every time I went to the Operating Room, I felt belittled on being asked by fellow colleagues as to how I would drape a patient. I felt my professional background and credibility were being questioned. Added to this agony were regular comments on my accent which made me more stressful. Burdened with unpleasant queries on the way I spoke, I had to learn to say that I spoke Queen's English, the credit for which I owe to a friend and colleague, Dr Lavin at the Cleveland Clinic. The loss of close family connections coupled with stressful situation, made me even more lonesome and I longed to be back in my home in Bombay. It was a very tough struggle for both me and my husband, often questioning our decision to leave India. With no Indian friends, initially, no Indian restaurants, we felt miserable in a place where even summer months of September felt like

winter for us. And even to get the Indian grocery seemed more of a chore for us – the nearest one was in Athens, Ohio. My husband, a qualified engineer from India, decided to study further. He completed his Masters degree in Industrial Engineering at Cleveland State University, while I pursued residency for two years which allowed me to take my Board Examination in Medicine in Philadelphia. It was in 1970 that we could begin to see a ray of hope for our new life in the US. In 1970, I got my Ohio license, a stepping stone to my medical career. With a three-and-a-half year old son, we needed to have extra financed to put him in a good school. Working in emergency shifts in two hospitals (St. John's and Fairview) simultaneously, helped us tide through this. In 1971, we bought a house on the east side, with my husband's prosperous position at General Electricals. At the same time, I got a job at Kaiser as an Officer In-charge of General Practice Outpatient. I also got an opportunity to teach medical students on a part-time basis at the Metro hospital. With the initial difficulties, it seemed well nigh impossible to establish a full fledged career along the same lines as I had in India. Trained in OB/GYN, I always wished to continue practice in this field. A position of senior resident came up when a senior resident was sacked at the Fairview Hospital and Cleveland Clinic. I was fortunate to get the job – which was not an ideal job in terms of the nature of the work it involved. I alternated between the two institutions, spending four months at Fairview and eight at the Clinic. At the end of my first four month work at Cleveland Clinic, I recall being summoned by my Chief who made me wary of the fact that as a foreign medical graduate and as a woman, this would be a very tough place for me as I would be under extreme pressure to perform well. With three men on board, I decided to accept the challenge after quitting from Kaiser. As a woman doctor and a foreigner, I was unable to get away from constant feeling and fear of being in a war zone trying to protect my identity, my gender and my Indian culture. A relentless struggle, as it may seem, looking back, I was proud to have proven myself in my career as a successful foreign medical graduate and a woman whose identity was defined by her perseverance and a culture that dictated hard work and success as the ultimate goals. I had a successful career at the Cleveland Clinic Foundation for 35 years until my retirement in 2000, although continuing part time until July 2010.

Dr Kamala Nagpaul hails from Delhi. She obtained her graduate and post graduate degrees in Economics from the University of Delhi and her degree in Education also from the University of Delhi. The Nagpauls got married in India in 1958, and came to the US in 1959. Although Dr Hans Nagpaul started his graduate degree at Bryn Mawr College in Philadelphia, his research on teenage pregnancies did not meet the approval of the authorities and he decided to quit and came to Cleveland in 1960 (Plate 23).

Plate 23

Dr Hans and Kamala Nagpaul came to Cleveland in 1960

Dr Kamala Nagpaul came to the US on a student visa, completed her Master's in Social Work at Bryn Mawr College in Philadelphia after which she worked at the children's services (foster care) who sponsored her application. She went back to India in March 1963 and worked as a social worker in the Department of Preventive and Social Medicine at the Lady Hardinge Medical College in Delhi. Although her immigration was approved in 1964, Dr Nagpaul was undecided about her big move to the US. While her friends in India persuaded her to come, it was not until about a year later that she left India to come to Cleveland to join her husband. With a string of successful degrees, Dr Nagpaul found herself highly qualified for jobs when several employing agencies rejected her applications. Marred by this frustration, she almost gave up when her first job against maternity leave at the Cleveland Society for the Blind provided her some hope of establishing a career. Although demanding, Dr Nagpaul's dedication and regular presentations at various seminars fetched her a regular job at the Society. It was not long before she got a permanent position at the Benjamin Roe Institute, a renowned gerontology government agency in Cleveland, in 1967 – a job she held until her retirement in 2001. Despite no retirement or pension benefits associated with her last job, Dr Nagpaul expresses a sense of satisfaction and achievement at her career of 34 years. She fondly recalls her travels around the world for various gerontological conferences which enriched her life both socially and professionally. Her involvement in issues of elder abuse and domestic violence won her respect and recognition at the national and international levels. As a proud mother of two boys, one a social worker and the other a physician, Dr Nagpaul's experiences speak of the trajectories of a successful woman – both professional and personal.

The above narratives, interesting as they may appear to the reader, are more than a great revelations of memories; they also relate to the degree of comfort with which to uncover their past and recall experiences, perhaps now in a different historical and geographical meaning. They also reveal cultural gaps in the early days of the emerging cultural diversity when issues of traditional costumes, food, religious attires and the Sikh turban (the religious headgear), were not only subject to subtle dissociation but also stirred a vying need for reinforcing cultural values.

Although some of the immigrant women who came to Cleveland in the 1960s and 1970s came as dependents of their husbands, they were educated professional women who successfully interfaced with a different socio-economic and socio-cultural environment. Their autonomy as mothers, wives and more importantly, as professional women leaves no void in our understanding of the choices and opportunities that exist in India today.

The first Asian Indians in Northeast Ohio have maintained a cultural continuity, at the same time have successfully accommodated a new one in a different socio-cultural milieu, or how else would they have left fascinating 'tales of success' for us to treasure and learn from – 'tales of success' which reveal both continuity and change have, undoubtedly paved the way for a deeper understanding of successive generations of Asian Indians from their perspective. This forms the subject matter of the following chapter.

Notes

1. Vijay Agnew (ed.), 2005, *Diaspora, Memory, and Identity: A Search for Home*, Toronto: University of Toronto Press, 21.
2. The term nostalgia derives from the Greek *nostos* which means 'to return home', and *algia* which means a 'painful feeling.' See Pamela Sugiman. 2005, 'Memories of Internment: Narrating Japanese-Canadian Women's Life's Stories,' in Vijay Agnew (ed.), *Diaspora, Memory, and Identity: A Search for Home*, Toronto: University of Toronto Press, 48–77, 63.

3. Gurharpal Singh, 2003, 'Introduction,' in Bhikhu Parekh, Gurharpal Singh and Steven Vertovec, *Culture and Economy in the Indian Diaspora*, London: Routledge, 1–12, 5.
4. Cynthia Miller, 2008, 'Immigrants, Images and Identity: Visualising Homelands Across Borders,' in Parvati Raghuram, Ajaya Sahoo et al. (eds), *Tracing an Indian Diaspora: Contexts, Memories, Representations*, New Delhi: Sage, 284–298, p. 287.
5. Personal communication with Dr Ashok and Dr Minal Pradhan, Cleveland, Ohio.
6. For an understanding of women's role as an agency in creating the transnational world, see Shobita Jain, 2010, 'Transmigrant Women's agency and Indian Diaspora,'*South Asian Diaspora*, 2 (2), 185–200, 185.
7. Dr V.N. Shirodkar was educated and trained in Bombay and London, and practiced Obstetrics and Gynaecology in his own hospital while teaching at the University of Bombay. He invented a Uterine stitch, later called the Shirodkar Operation stitch which helped women to complete their pregnancy allowing successful deliveries. He gained accolades for his discovery and became popular in India and internationally. He was invited by the University Hospitals to demonstrate this new technique. It is believed that Sophia Loren, after two unfortunate miscarriages, and hearing about Dr Shirodkar's expertise, flew him to Rome to perform the required operation., which was successful; later, she had a son with Carlos Ponti. The news was also picked up by Time Magazine.
8. A renowned gynaecologist known for his Shirodkar operation stitch.
9. A political leader, the first Indian High Commissioner to Britain after Indian Independence in 1947, a close associate of Jawaharlal Nehru, and Defence Minister under Jawaharlal Nehru's Prime Ministership.
10. Indian diplomat and politician, and sister of the first Prime Minister of independent India, Jawaharlal Nehru.
11. Personal discussions with Mr Sham Gautam.
12. Cynthia J. Miller, 2008, 'Immigrants, Images and Identity: Visualising Homelands Across Borders,' in Parvati Raghuram, Ajaya Sahoo et al. (eds), 2008, New Delhi: Sage, 264–98, 286.

13. The Lotus, March 1968 (6), 1. See also P. Bala, October 2013, 'Asian Indians: Significant Highlights of the Community in northeast Ohio,' *The Encyclopedia of Cleveland History,* Cleveland.
14. *Dewans* or service is the desire to inform others about Indian culture and customs (remark by Ajeet Singh Sood, *The Cleveland Press*, 17 May 1965, p. 3.
15. Personal communication with Ajeet Singh Sood.
16. For details, see Poonam Bala, October 2013, 'Asian Indians – Significant Highlights of the Community in northeast Ohio,' *The Encyclopedia of Cleveland History,* Cleveland.
17. With the increasing scope of activities of the India House Project, the India House was renamed the India Community Center in 1977.
18. Information about Paramjit Singh has been obtained from clevelandpeople.com
19. For details, see clevelandpeople.com website which honors individuals annually for their efforts in promoting the value of the 'tossed salad' of diversity which makes Cleveland a richer city.

CHAPTER 4

'New' Identity and 'Old' Institutions

Voices and Viewpoints

Arranged Marriages in India – 'antiquated, and unacceptable.'

Social and Religious Customs in India – 'how can they still survive? How can they be relevant in this century'?

The above are recorded remarks and reactions of some of the second generation Asian Indians in Northeast Ohio. The persistence of institutionalized marriages in India is looked upon with surprise coupled with apologies for those experiencing them.

The establishment of a unique identity in their adopted homeland has several implications for Asian Indians in the US. As Gittschlich remarks,

> Indian Americans may well make sure that their voice will be heard when it comes to issues such as immigration and naturalization, family unification, discrimination, hate crimes, and racist violence, education, health care, or business interests.[1]

While language, religion and other social institutions symbolize the traditional values of ethnicity, they also act as instruments resisting change, assimilation and loss of ethnic values in a new social environment. Embedded in countries of origin, they also legitimize the very existence of social and ethnic groups in a new society. The integration of the Indian community in America, generally, and in Ohio, more specifically, in Northeast Ohio, can be seen as a dynamic process engaging resistance and accommodation both of which created new commitments to the American ways of living. While an ethnic social group may reinvent and modify traditional values to maintain or even to create a new ethnic identity, language is held as the main symbol of the new identity. While an ethnic community is not always marked by a linguistic community,

> in a multi-ethnic society characterized by cultural contentions, language could become an important element of ethnic identity.[2]

Nonetheless, the traditional linguistic system may suffer attrition as a result of the secondary significance accorded in western cultures. Following are some compelling anecdotes of second generation Asian Indian student community which indicate an abyss in the knowledge of the language of their mother tongue. They also indicate a need to understand the role of the language in daily social interactions.

> At home, we speak a mix of Tamil and English, says S. Among the extended family, we usually speak in Tamil. When my brother and I were younger, there was definitely pressure from our parents to speak in Tamil for they were concerned that we would lose our ability to speak our mother tongue if we spoke in English at school and at home. Besides, I am really proud that I can speak in my mother tongue, even though I am not completely fluent. I become self-conscious of this limitation when I am with family friends who speak in Tamil. I can read

> and write at the basic level but could not go any further as my grandmother, who took great pains to teach me, passed away and I lost that connection.

S's parents are originally from the State of Tamil Nadu in India. Her father grew up in Coimbatore and her mother in Salem. Her father obtained a Bachelors degree in Engineering in India and later earned a Doctorate in Information Systems at the University of Houston. Her mother is also a graduate from a reputed institution, Indian Institute of Science in Bangalore and accompanied her father to America to seek better opportunities for higher education.

RM's father was born in Pakistan before the partition after which her family moved to Moradabad. He wanted to study for engineering but owing to health reasons was unable to write the entrance examination and instead got convinced by a friend to try for medicine where he obtained the highest score. He finished his medical training and continued graduate studies in Orthopedics. Family pressures for marriage, however, dissuaded him from pursuing his residency in England. After marriage to RM's mother, a teacher at Maharani College in Jaipur, RM's father went to England, completed his residency and came to New York to do another residency which fetched him a suitable job in Ohio. Having grown up in a household where Hindi was spoken by both parents, RM, sees no issues of language in her home. She remarks,

> we speak a mix of Hindi and English. There is no pressure to speak in any of the languages. I am very grateful to my parents for teaching me my mother tongue. I cannot read it but it is very helpful to be able to speak in Hindi and Punjabi.

It is evident that the issue of language is of major significance, especially amongst the second generation Asian Indians. There is a perceived consciousness either to be able to or not to be able to carry a conversation in the language of their mother tongue. Here is what another student, KK, has to say:

> I speak to my parents in English entirely. At home, though, my mother – many times – speaks to me in Marathi while I respond in English. My father hardly speaks to me in Marathi. My parents still speak Marathi but speak in English when we have guests who are unable to speak in Marathi. Although I can also Converse fluently in Marathi, I am not as confident speaking it as I am in English which can be frustrating,

R's father was born in Lahore before partition but grew up in Haryana (Sonipat) where his family moved after partition in 1947. He came to the US in 1967 to pursue a Masters degree at Johns Hopkins University and also got an MBA from George Washington University. He went back to India in 1973 to marry R's mother who grew up in Jabalpur (Madhya Pradesh). Thus, although grew up in a Hindi and Punjabi-speaking household, she almost laments the fact that she is not fluent in her native tongue. She presents herself as being very keen on learning both Hindi and Punjabi.

> I grew up with my parents speaking to me in Hindi, and I would respond in English. I think I have been a bit resentful of that point. But in general, I feel that Hindu Punjabi parents make less of an effort to teach their children Hindi/Punjabi than their Gujarati/South Indian counterparts. It was not until I worked in rural India for two years in my twenties that I picked up Hindi. Even now I have to make an effort to speak Hindi with my parents – they will not push me to do so. While traveling to South Asia, initially, I felt inadequate about not being able to speak but am now very confident and pleased that I can travel independently and mix freely with my friends and relations in India.

While second and third generation children may occasionally express a degree of inaptness in not knowing their mother tongue, they also face no problem in knowing the basics to get by during family meetings, as MK, says,

> I speak English at home with my parents and Gujarati and English among members of my father's family.

MK's father is Gujarati but was born and raised in Burma until age 10, after which he went to Bombay to pursue his High School and College education. Higher education was the main reason for his move to America.

Recalling one of my classes and my interaction with Asian Indian students, I was struck by the sudden lack of motivation of a very sincere student, MR in class-participation the reason for which, I later found out was MR's limited knowledge of MR's mother tongue. Distressed by this limitation, MR, had to run from pillar to post to find books to learn her mother tongue. Yet, when MR finally went to her parents' home country, the joy of visiting her relations for the first time, was marred by MR's inability to communicate with them. MR's parents were both professionals but chose to speak with their children in English.

Being closest to the cultural practices of their parents, often from first generation, the second generation children have made conscious efforts to identify themselves as being part of India and one way of doing this was through language connections. This also corroborates the significance of language and culture for minority families which

> is at the centre of key debates about assimilation, integration, cohesion, citizenship, multiculturalism, and racial and ethnic identity.[3]

NN's family hails from Orissa and came to the US after her mother's relatives sponsored her family. NN was 5 months old, and her brother was 6 years when they came. Their move to the US opened up several opportunities for her father to do his residency as a physician. There were not as many other families from Orissa, as there were from states like Gujarat, Punjab, and Andhra Pradesh. NN's family settled in New York, which was a melting pot for diverse cultures which facilitated the initial process of settling in a new culture. For NN, language means a lot in terms of retaining a distinct identity, as evident from the following:

> We came from the state of Orissa, on the eastern coast of India. So the native tongue was Oriya. At home my parents spoke in Oriya which helped me learn my parents's language a lot faster. When I was older, I made a concerted effort to learn the language and be comfortable speaking it. I noticed that other kids who were born and brought up here had a better command of the language with their grand-parents residing with them. Words, sentences and colloquialism flowed much more smoothly with that influence at the home. Needless to say, I enjoyed speaking in Oriya with my relatives back home for it formed a bond of similar identity and connections.

Lack of cultural familiarity and cultural identification is closely linked with a limited knowledge of mother tongue and this comes out clearly in most second and third generation Asian Indians, as indicated below by M.

> My parents primarily converse in Marathi, though my mother grew up speaking Konkani. My mother's parents came to live with us after my older brother was born in 1975 and although they spoke Konkani to each other, they only spoke to me and my brother in English. Perhaps, my parents and grandparents were concerned about us speaking in more than one language which they thought would confuse us later in our growing years. I do, however, deeply regret this as often I feel disconnected with my culture. I have always been upset about my inability to communicate with relatives in their language which almost compels them to accommodate my limitations of

> speaking in their language. I feel deprived of a significant cultural experience by not being able to engage with them in their language. One of the most rewarding and stimulating experiences a person can have is by visiting a country and being able to experience the world through their eyes, with language as the main vehicle for achieving this ambition. However, I have always felt that my limitations in speaking the language have prevented me from doing this whenever I have visited India and although as an Asian Indian, I can have a great opportunity to serve as a cultural ambassador between the two worlds, my limitations in spoken language of my parents have marred this future vision of mine.

While a lot of first generation parents try to communicate with their children in their mother tongue, sometimes an overemphasis on this poses a barrier to acquiring English language skills. K, for instance shares an incident which he says, might have influenced language learning issues in his family.

> At home we speak a mix of Tamil and English. My mother speaks almost exclusively in Tamil, especially since her language skills improved after living in rural Tamil Nadu for a year. I speak exclusively in English. My father speaks to us mostly in English interspersed with Tamil phrases and words. I communicate in Tamil to my aunts and grandmother, but use English with all my uncles and cousins. Although my Tamil is fairly good, my English is slightly better. When I was very young, I was encouraged to speak Tamil, but since my sister had trouble communicating, her teacher suggested to my parents to adopt English as the language of communication at home. It was probably at that time that our mother tongue became secondary and we almost lost track of it over the years. As for issues relating to travel to India, I can convey my thoughts when needed, in Tamil, but my accent will always be different to a native speaker. Nevertheless, it helps me connect with my family.

The Institution of Marriage

India has had a long tradition of institutionalized arranged marriages, usually initiated by the prospective bride and groom's parents. Economic and social standing and caste, form the basis of these negotiations. Owing to their caste and economic class associations, the practice of arranged marriages occasionally poses a formidable barrier to alliances between members of different castes. The caste system originated several thousands of years back in India, with the most lucid definition offered by M.N. Srinivas, a renowned Indian anthropologist, as

> a hereditary, endogamous, usually localized group, having traditional association with an occupation, and a particular position in the hierarchy of castes. Relations between castes are governed, among other things, by the concepts of pollution, and purity, and generally maximum commensality occurs within the caste.[4]

India is a country where social hierarchy over the years has been defined by caste groups represented by the *Brahmans, Kshatriyas, Vaisyas, Sudras* and the scheduled castes or Dalit, renamed by Mahatma Gandhi as *harijan* or 'people of God.' In the 1970s, the definition of Dalits was extended to include scheduled tribes, neo-Buddhists, the working people, the landless and poor peasants, women and all those who are being exploited politically, economically and in the name of religion.[5]

A majority of Asian Indian students questioned the validity of caste as an institution, often describing it as 'antiquated and unacceptable.' This was often remarked in the light of the fact that physical appearance, beauty and colour were considered indispensable to a successful marriage alliance.

> Skin colour as a legacy of the subcontinent's past has shaped and continues to shape South Asians' cultural perceptions of beauty, identity, and difference. Indeed, the pressure on

families to have fair offspring in some cases begins before the baby is born, is illustrated by such family practices as giving the expectant mother milk mixed with saffron to drink during her pregnancy.[6]

This is a traditional way of ensuring the birth of a 'fair 'or light-complexioned child. A common response that emerged from various accounts reflects on their perception of the system, which reveals more surprise than an understanding and easy acceptance. Continuing with the above quotes, following are expressions of disagreements of second generation Asian Indian with 'traditional' modes of life style in India. In as much as the anecdotes may seem 'reactionary,' and explicitly expressive, they seen to be based on cogent reasons provided by them.

While most second and third generation Asian Indians were unable to fathom the continuity of the caste system in India, they also had limited knowledge of its functionalities in the twentieth century – for them, caste was not only limiting but also a major obstacle to social activities. AP, with a firsthand experience working amongst the less privileged groups in India laments the system as follows:

> In India, I'd spent time with small and marginal farmers facing difficulties in producing enough food to avoid a life of starvation. While it is not so easy to lay caste as a charge on the reasons why many poor, itinerant farmers have trouble maintaining land and water rights as well as access to affordable inputs, I will say, that it was my experience to have seen a lot of these people form the excluded, lower castes. Progressive legislation is not, and never will be, the problem in India. But social ills in rural areas, including discrimination based on caste still exists. Many of the farmers I met had lost their lands due to multi-national takeovers. By and large, vast tracts of land that are sold to multi-nationals in India are lands inhabited by tribal and low caste people. It is, of course, not a one-sided issue. The government has implemented reforms in

> areas of government and academic quotas for Scheduled Tribes (STs) and Other Backward Castes (OBCs). Yet, it's my belief, that violation of social and economic rights occurs in many of the country's unseen, under reported areas, and it is the practice of exclusion that has, in part, stifled the realization of India's progressive democratic policies.

Speaking of the caste system, on a similar note, R remarks that,

> I could never live in India for this reason. It is very hard for me to justify all the hard labour that is done in India without getting compensated. Everyone has a servant, driver, maid and other helpers for household work. People who live there are dependent on their servants and mock at me for doing everyday stuff such as doing my own dishes or mowing my own lawn. I feel very independent here in the US. I can go wherever and whenever I want and don't have to worry about my driver. I can cook my own food the way I like it and I even enjoy mowing my own lawn.

Besides, KR sees no issue in the existence of caste system in India. As he states,

> I never spoke about caste system until I went to India. I was struck by the extent to which caste can be stifling to career prospects in rural India, although it is seemingly less relevant in urban India. It has no impact at all on my life here.

While caste, education and economic status divide the Indian society into different echelons, the institution of arranged marriages in India has been in existence since long. Issues of agreements and disagreements loomed large over ideas of 'love,' strangeness amongst couples, and the underlying differences in the personalities, or 'the chemistry' between the couple. The following opinions reveal the extent to which conflicts ensue between first and second generation Asian Indians when it comes to finding a suitable spouse for their children.

> I think before we began to 'look' for my older brother, says S, my parents assumed that both of us would get into an arranged marriage. They are currently looking for a girl for my brother. It is not just a basic on-paper compatibility that people are willing to settle for ... everyone seeks love and basic compatibility. When we began to look for a wife for my brother, I made it clear to my parents that I had no interest in going for marriage with someone I do not know. The only stipulation my father gave me was that I would not be allowed to have a Hindu wedding if I brought home a White boy, Black boy, or any other boy but Hindu. He also affirmed his presence without disrespecting our traditional customs. Since it has taken them long to find a suitable bride for my brother, their only concern for me is to find one at the right age and time failing which they will be compelled to find one for me.

The social institution of caste does not play the same role of social differentiation amongst the Indian community in Northeast Ohio as in India. While caste may still be significant for some when identifying and defining prospective marriage partners, its role is underplayed in social interactions not only in Ohio but also in other States in America. Perhaps, it is because of the understated significance that the responses indicate little or limited knowledge of exactly 'what it does in the Indian context.'

So remarks one:

> I would say I have a generally good understanding of the caste system. It does not play a major role in daily life but there is no great reason to point out what caste you are or make it obvious to others. It does not limit my social relations at all here – in fact, many of my Asian Indian friends do not even know what caste they belong to. However, if I were to have an arranged marriage, my parents would definitely only look for one within our caste.

Yet another remark from AP on marriage and caste corroborates the above issues.

> My parents, of course, had an arranged marriage. I do not think it is as easy to say 'I believe in arranged marriage' or 'I do not.' My parents were not forced to marry each other. Each of them had a choice; my mother had the upper hand in that regard. What is important is mutual respect and equality in decision on marriage. I think part of the misconception on the matter arises from the fact that we conflate the idea of 'arranged' with 'forced.' And this happens in India as well as to a certain extent amongst the Asian Indian community in the US too. My parents would ideally want me to marry a Hindu girl but I am flexible on this. I have dated white American girls and Indian girls and have also introduced my parents to an American girl on one occasion with no issues whatsoever but regretfully, it did not result in marriage.

While parents see some advantages in having an arranged marriage for their children, the latter see it as less significant, yet proving beneficial with parental intervention in terms of negotiations. AP sees concepts of dating and marriage thereafter as a learning process but also respects the relevance of arranged marriages in the Indian context and both for him and his parents, caste is not relevant when it comes to choosing a partner. While choosing a caste-specific spouse may not be important to some, others view it as beneficial often surrounded with expressions of curiosity than its mere 'rejection' or 'acceptance' as evident from RM's statement as follows:

> On the issue of marriage, my parents have an open mind and they accepted the fact that they brought us to this country to give us a better life, which also exposes us to the possibility of bringing someone home that is not Indian. We grew up in a very small town in the middle of nowhere in Ohio with approximately 8 Indian families and I also ended up going to a rural

University where you could count the number of Indians. Somehow, my sister and I found our roots when it was time to get married since we both ended up marrying Indians. Arranged marriage is also about meeting your partner on the internet which is very common today. When I asked my parents about their arranged marriage and how they did it, my mother's response was 'we didn't know anything else. In the US, people date forever, get married, get bored with each other and then get divorced. In India, we date after we get married and learn to love the other person.' Arranged marriages definitely work for many people but it is definitely not for me. I am a very outgoing person who was hoping to meet that special person that compliments me, luckily I did end up meeting that person. However, if I had not met him, I would have accepted an arranged marriage. Fortunately, I didn't have to argue with my parents for they allowed me the freedom of choice. I respect their feelings which does not affect any of my social relations.

For KR and his parents, caste has not meant anything majorly significant.

My parents never gave importance to caste. There used to be an organization that focused on bringing together young people from specific castes in a scheduled venue where they could mingle and take decisions accordingly at a later stage; but that seems to have fallen apart as the community is too small.

Here is another perspective of arranged marriages, by M.

My parents themselves had a mixed marriage and arranged marriage was out of the question. As a teenage girl, I had to follow very stringent rules for socialization. My freedom was restricted, but after I left for college I was free to do as I liked and my parents never pressured me in any way about my personal life. I don't understand how any young person today could want an arranged marriage but I realize family pressure

> can be immense and I have heard young women in India wish mostly for economic security, even wealth, from a partner their parents would find.

While for NN, marriage was not only 'a tabooed' issue at home, it was never taken up as an important issue for discussion. Here is a case which involves a clear conflict between the first generation parents and their children.

> Marriage was never emphasized as a goal. It was not discussed even in general whimsical terms such as 'when you get married … .' It was just not a topic of discussion. Having a career and being able to support myself was the path, everything else will come later. Modesty was also a factor. My parents always discouraged me from having any type of relationships with the opposite sex. On the same note, arranged marriage was never a topic of discussion. It was never assumed that a groom would be chosen for me nor was I raised to believe so. I think my parents assumed that I would want to marry an Indian because I was raised with Indian cultural values and traditions. But that presented many discrepancies. What exactly was 'our culture'? Coming from a less represented subculture (Oriya) provided much less interaction with our specific customs, language, etc. I had friends from all over but I mostly interacted with Punjabis, Gujaratis or Sindhis. And I noticed differences in the way their households were compared to mine. For example, their cultures seemed much iess conservative and had more social functions that were both religious and non-religious by nature. They also seemed to congregate more and had more of an organised social network for adults and children. My friends from these cultures seemed more apt to socialize with Indians and that network made them feel most comfortable. Being in school was one kind of network, but their other social network comprised of Indians they would meet with, on the weekends or after school. I was different in this respect because I felt comfortable with any culture both inside and outside of school.

> And I didn't feel necessarily compelled to be a part of the Indian social network. The only thing that made it easier was that Indians understood the restrictions of strict parents, whereas Americans did not and it was humiliating and embarrassing at times as an adolescent. My home culture and life were so conservative that I wasn't even allowed to take dance classes, for it meant performance and display against the standard of humility and modesty; nonetheless, I was allowed to wear make up and to listen to whatever music I wanted to.

The views of first and second generation Asian Indians on arranged marriages, thus, offer different perspectives. While some see it as a totally viable and successful institution in practice, others deny the practicality in terms of lack of familiarity. Yet, despite a personal belief in its legitimacy, most second generation Indians in Northeast Ohio opt out of it. With no value judgments in place, it indicates a subtle acceptance of arranged marriage as an institution, as M describes.

> I have always seen my parents as progressive when it came to dating and marriage, as they never pressured me to date a certain girl. I recently got married to an American girl this past October and my parents were very supportive of the alliance and were delighted in meeting and getting to know my wife's family. I suspect this is one advantage to the way my parents raised me in that I was always free to explore various options and didn't feel inhibited by cultural expectations; I was raised as an American after all. My parents' relationship was unique in that they were the only ones in their respective family not to have an arranged marriage. Perhaps, this influenced their progressive attitude towards dating and marriage, which they extended to me and my brother. I think arranged marriages can work and I have certainly seen instances of their success, including that of my aunts and uncles. One of the benefits of arranged marriages is that it lays a foundation of common ground and mutual understanding between two families which

> is important for any successful marriage. Seen in that light, I don't have a problem with arranged marriages. After all, in the US where 'love marriages' are more frequently practised, the divorce rate is above 50 per cent, which hardly testifies to the superiority of this system over arranged marriages.

There is a degree of flexibility in accepting the American system of dating prior to marriage, as evident from KR's statement.

> My parents are fine with dating now but were not supportive while we were in high school. In college, they were mostly concerned that we focus on grades and not on socializing. My view of arranged marriage is that it can work so long as both parties are open to it without being coerced into it. Personally, I would only opt for this if I happen to be single and unattached by the time I am 35 and that's just because I value my freedom of choice.

Education

While education indicates a social status and acceptance, sometimes it has undertones of gender differences. For instance, RB felt that

> My parents definitely view education as important but see it differently in terms of my brother and I (with me, marriage is more of a concern). Also, my parents also view education as a status symbol; therefore when they think about education they look at the 'caliber' of the school as a measure of how potentially intelligent someone else.

S recalls how her parents always encouraged her to go for higher education at the same time gave her freedom to opt for a career of her choice.

> Education has always been an important aspect of my life. I don't think I ever doubted that I would go to college … or

continue on and do some sort of graduate/professional school. It was always just a matter of which professional path I would choose. On this note, I have felt very little pressure from my parents.

While always encouraging me to be the best (not to DO my best, but to BE the best), when I did occasionally do poorly (by our greatly inflated standards), they never got upset with me or disappointed. I have always been independent when it came to doing my homework or working on my projects. My parents never interfered with what grades I was getting on each test, unless I brought it to their attention. They assumed I'd get an A grade. In terms of my extended family, they wouldn't know where I was going to school and how good (or bad) the school was, unless it was Harvard or Yale. Other than that, all the schools must be the same, in their eyes. This definitely irks me. I think it will change when my cousins' kids get to be old enough to be looking at universities. My parents and I have not really had any great conflicts over my career choice. My brother is and always wanted to be a doctor – a typical career for our generation, but he was never pushed into it. In fact, my parents would have been happy if he had gone on to graduate school in chemistry or taken the offer he got from Procter and Gamble for a job. Of course, my father pointed out that it may be difficult to live the comfortable lifestyle I am used to on an anthropologist's salary. They didn't even flinch when I very seriously considered pursuing a PhD in classics and becoming a classics professor. He has always been an advocate of hard sciences, so once it became clear that I was interested in psychology, he began to push for neuroscience. I think, he simply wants me to have a strong foundation in the biology and neuroscience behind the more intangible ideas that I plan to study (memory, etc.). Indian parents have a major role in guiding their children about the educational path they 'ought to follow.'

And this continues in some of the first generation Asian Indians in Cleveland. Here is a slightly different perspective for Rimmy.

> My parents view education as a must and say you can not get anywhere in this world without it. I am very fortunate that I have parents with an open mind. A lot of Asian parents force their children to be doctors. My parents gave me the freedom to do whatever I wanted to as long as I could support myself in the long run. In India, I don't think education per se is a status symbol, but the amount of money you have and how you flaunt it around. Many of the business families make a lot more money than the average doctors and lawyers and they are looked upon as higher status symbol, where as the majority of Asian parents in the US expect their children to be doctors, lawyers and engineers.

In almost all Asian Indian homes, education is considered to be of utmost significance. In discussing her situation, NN recalls,

> My father was the sole breadwinner in the home, though my mother started working part-time when I was 6. She did this to gain some type of financial independence, which later manifested in her earning her Associates, Bachelors, and Masters degrees at a later age. She was married at 19, though had completed a basic undergraduate education in Nutrition in India. Education was valued above all other aspects, including physical appearance, athletics, social life, etc. Academic success was the only way to be praised in our household. Anything that came in the way of a focus on academic standards, was looked down upon. The humanities were always looked at as without having weight or substance, particularly by my mother. My father had an appreciation for arts and letters but did not have respect for such as a discipline. The only thing they wanted from us was to do well and become doctors, which me nor my brother, ended up doing.

Sometimes, education for first generation Indians meant education in a high ranking school and with a professional career path. However, for M, his parents were far from interfering in his choice of career.

> With respect to education, I have often felt an intense pressure to achieve good grades and also the highest. For my parents, good grades was a means to reap significant rewards in America. (One consequence of this 'grades-first' mentality is that it led me to prize the letter grade above the process of learning for the sake of my own personal edification. As a result, I commonly looked for ways to get a high grade, even if it came at the expense of investing considerable time in the learning process). Whereas many kids in America are satisfied and proud to graduate from college, I always felt that the name and ranking of the school was most commonly emphasised. In other words, getting a university education was not sufficient, you had to graduate from a sufficiently high ranked school to feel any sense of accomplishment. Much like athletics is seen by inner-city kids in America as a means to achieveing success, South Asian culture commonly equates academic achievement with economic advancement. In any case, I give my parents a lot of credit for their willingness to allow me to pursue my own career goals. Although they pressurized me to achieve academically, they never emphasized one profession over another, which I know many of my friends' parents did. For instance, there was much less credibility attached to professions outside of the medical, legal or engineering fields in the Indian community where I grew up (in Toledo, Ohio). My parents, however, were very much opposed to this limited vision.

Ashwin recalls the difficult times his parents shared with him while in his growing years. Education meant a lot to his parents, even if it meant sacrificing families and friends in India. With both parents physicians, emigrating from India was a result of economic necessity and family bindings. So Ashwin recalls,

I grew up in a small town. There wasn't much to do. Our school system was poor as were many of the people who lived there. Not many people went to college after high school. We were a thriving town in the early twentieth century, home to the world's largest manufacturer of ceramics. This kept us afloat even during the depression. Located in the Ohio Valley on the borders of Ohio, West Virginia and Pennsylvania, the area's steel factories and coal mines kept us working, moneyed, and fed. But the collapse of the American steel industry in the seventies changed all of that. My family moved there in the eighties, at the beginning of that decline. Teenage pregnancy was high. The dropout rate too was high. Drugs were not uncommon. Poor whites and all of the town's blacks lived in economically depressed East End. Growing up, people would ask, 'What are you going to do next?' as opposed to something like 'Where are you going to college?' This is to say that a general decline in the quality of town life may have precipitated certain failures in our school system. I can't say for sure. But I was sheltered from these things because my parents encouraged – in fact, went at great lengths to engage me in – activities that required learning. Mostly, my love of books. I won't say they were stingy with money, but the only things they outright agreed to buy me – without fail – were books. It didn't matter what subject: The Beatles, John F. Kennedy, The Bernstein Bears, Judy Blume books, Charles Shultz Charlie Brown books, books on plants, history and atlases. My mother is a family doctor in that town so she knew people directly involved in my school life: teachers, nurses, lunchroom workers, students, custodians, etc. She monitored my learning by exposing me to books but also by keeping tabs on me through some of her patients. By the end of the eighth grade it was apparent that I would not be able to attend the area high school. The school system was crumbling. Due to a decrease in the population, the school was losing funding. Teacher salaries were cut and of course, many of the good ones left. I didn't want to leave that town. My friends were there. But my parents

> decided to send me to a private school in Wheeling, West Virginia, called The Linsly School which was a military school (in the early twentieth century). But by the time I joined, it was a co-ed college prep school with a fledgling reputation.

KR expressed satisfaction in pursuing what he thought was right in doing, despite his parents' wishes for a career. He remarks

> I completed a BA in Economics from Case Western Reserve University and have mild ambitions of getting an MBA, so I don't really fit into the mould of most people of Indian decent. My parents are outwardly very supportive of the decisions I have made, but I know they wish I would have sought a more prestigious track for myself. But I've made peace with myself for living my own life.

Status of Women: Some Viewpoints

Comparing the status of women in the US with those in India, and seeing it in the perspective of education, independence, choice of partner in marriage, several viewpoints emerged.

As R says,

> when I see my parents' marriage I see a major difference in my mother's role vs. that of American women. My mother sacrificed much more and accepted a traditional role in the household than other mothers I've seen. When I lived in rural India, I was shocked by the subservient role women played in society – almost confined to the household, doing domestic chores wearing a veil, among other things.

For RM too, Indian women have a long way to go before they can be on par with women in America when it comes to making independent choices for a decent living.

> Unfortunately, the status of women in India is still behind the times and has not caught up with US yet. It is slowly easing up

> but it will take a while to catch up. Many people in India still live in joint families and the new daughter-in-law is expected to act a certain way and do certain things which is very limiting. Many of them are expected to give up their careers so they can be mothers even though they have multiple nannies taking care of their children.

M feels fortunate not having been born and raised in India where a majority of women face discrimination with no freedom because of their gender, he thinks.

> I am so grateful to be a woman with citizenship in an advanced Western country where women have far more freedom and advantages than is the case generally in India – not that there isn't plenty of discrimination against women in the West as well – but I would never have had the freedom I do if I was born, raised and settled in India.

Speaking of the status of women in India, as a result of the close ties with India, second and third generation Indians in Northeast Ohio become part of the ongoing incidents in India – they feel dismayed at what their female cousins, relatives and friends go through in terms of 'forced marriages,' or other social issues. M narrates one such incidence about his family cousin in India:

> From my experience, women in America seem to be much less inhibited when it comes to making choices about anything from clothing to relationships to choices of school to attend. Whereas it has always seemed to me that Indian women are commonly pressured by their parents and families to carry themselves a certain way so as to not embarrass the family. For instance, one of my cousins recently moved from India to Canada after having an arranged marriage to a chef, who had advertized himself as having all the right credentials (decent salary, relatively fair skinned, proper caste – I think). Without really verifying this information, my cousin's family in India

> agreed to the marriage under the assumption that their daughter would be well off and, therefore, preserve the family reputation back home. To my dismay, much of what he advertized proved exaggerated as he wasn't nearly as wealthy or established as he had claimed. My cousin probably wouldn't have been allowed to come to North America had she not been married owing to restrictions and the stigma attached to a single-woman coming travelling abroad – at least this still seems to be the case in many families in India. Marriage, thus, seems to be foisted onto women in India, whereas American women seem to have much more freedom in deciding when and whom to marry.

KR has a similar opinion on women in India and in the US.

> I feel that the greatest difference is that despite being educated, women face several hurdles in all aspects of social interactions. In US Indian homes, I see less of this and this results in an empowerment of a completely different kind where identity can supercede education, etc. On the other hand, US-based Indian women friends of mine have complained about Indian men expecting them to cook and clean for them much as their mothers did. For this reason, some are more open to marrying non-Indians in order to have the kind of life which they think they deserve.

Best Part of being Indian or American

While there remain several stories to tell as also places to remember, both of which represent of a past vision of homeland, a link between geographical space and identity always occupy a central place in the personal experiences and lives of all individuals. The notion of being Indian or being American, has always been a difficult one to address, yet has been identified with grace by the second generation Asian Indians. R feels proud of being part of a culture that is so strong and has enlightened her. As a result, her identity is marked by both America and

India although the latter was strengthened only after her visit to India. On the contrary, SH was not sure of what really to say about these issues. She recalls,

> as a kid, my favorite part of being Indian was all the great food and my summer trips to India. As a teenager, my favorite part of being Indian was still all the great food and then, all the great clothes. At some point during my teenage years, it became really cool to be Indian and everything Indian became trendy. But, it was as a college student that I really explored my own Indian-ness (and how that mixed with being American) on my own, without being defined by my family. And since, I have embraced all that being Indian has given me – I love being bilingual, I love my skin tone, I love Hindi movies, I love being associated with (while completely inept at) so many interesting and beautiful types of dance, I love having more Indian 'formal' clothing than 'western' ones, I love realizing more and more that each part of India is unique with its own traditions and culture and I love being able to identify those qualities and differences and yet see how all of us second generation Indian kids have adapted and adopted them. And yes, I still absolutely love the food, especially, now that I can make more of it. And I think I am both American and Indian. I can never de-identify as Indian; my skin gives me away and the moment I open my mouth, the mixture of sarcasm, and an American accent gives away that I'm no Indian girl either. My parents made a clear effort to bring my brother and me up as having many Indian values as well as American ones. I love my heritage and am very proud of it. It definitely defines a good deal of who I am – but it is not that I am Indian or American – it is that I am BOTH. I have realized that it is a pretty unique experience, one that even all of us second generation kids don't really share in all the same ways.

Perhaps the best part of having Indian roots, says M, is that

> I find myself increasingly empathetic towards other immigrants and I don't take my citizenship for granted. I know

> that it wasn't easy for my parents to come to this country and from my visits to India, I have had the benefit of seeing how much of the world lives outside the United States. Whereas I find many Americans are largely ignorant of the world outside these borders, I feel at least somewhat culturally sensitive. And I feel I am more American than Indian because of my limited ties with India. Although, as a child I enjoyed reading about Indian mythology and delighted in attending pujas (worship) and other important ceremonies, I have not really maintained this practice as I have gotten older. Nevertheless, I do take pride in being Indian and having roots outside of America.

The exotic cultural representations of India go a long way in drawing the Asian Indian community in Northeast Ohio to India. For M, what is best about India is the closeness of family, wonderful food, colors, textiles. Issues of self-identity, cultural identity and expectations become obvious whenever first generation parents have tried to instill the same values in their children born in America. NN, for instance, narrates how her social interaction and expectations were influenced by her American and Indian network of friends.

> As a young adult, I realised the many expectations and stereotypes that were passed on to our generation within the Indian community, despite being born and brought up here in a multicultural setting. Many of my peers held the same views as their parents. This was even more so represented when I began my undergraduate career in the midwest. The attitudes and mentality of those I encountered were much more colloquial and they seemed to cling to their ethnicity with much more desperation than people in New York. Perhaps, this was due to the fact of so many cultures being represented and accepted, that people felt a little more comfortable in their own skin than those in the midwest who may have been one of the only Indian families in the area. The only thing that made it easier was that Indians understood the restrictions of strict parents,

> whereas Americans did not and it was humiliating and embarrassing at times as an adolescent.

For KR, the issue of feeling more American than Indian or vice versa has interesting correlation with identity presentation in India.

> I think it's important to understand what it's not like to be an American and to understand other perspectives from this world. India specifically teaches us important lessons of a dynamic 'kichidi' (like a melting pot) lifestyle as well as 'jugaad' (change as per needs). A certain openness of soul is required to fit in India and I think that openness allows one to be happy in many environments. I would identify myself as closer to America. I feel more comfortable here. I don't have the openness of soul that I mention above. That's why I moved back.

Besides, for S,

> identity is being defined by cultural affinity. For instance, she identifies with the arts, food and heritage of India at least as much as she does with the arts, food and heritage of America. There is also the social dynamic of culture that comes from association with peer groups outside of one's family.

Both Chetan and Akshar, connect with India through their parents, both of whom are successful professionals from India. Through short-term work opportunities in non-governmental organizations in India, today Chetan is proud of having experienced his culture and roots more deeply. And Akshar enjoys the elaborate and colorful festivities, especially Indian weddings.

> I love the food and rich colors people wear. They are quite different and better, than the 'black and white' weddings I have seen here. One thing that makes me sad though is that I see a lot of children on the streets who do not go to school. They ask for money and I want them to learn to read and write.

Thus, while there are several elements that provide a common feeling of distinctiveness with a common cultural base and history, these are often limited to first generation Indian communities. Amongst the several social institutions, for the nearly 85 per cent of people of Indian origin overseas,

> Hinduism is an 'ethnic religion' that is characterized by a strong sense of 'rooted ness in India.'[7]

Regular visits to temples, prayers, and observing Hindu festivals as a community have added to this sense of commonality amongst the Asian Indian communities. For the second and third generations, however, transnational connection with India are developed with native language skills. Although language, for them, provides a base on which they can try to discover their Indian roots, it also impedes complete acceptance in the subcontinent as a result of lack of, or even incomplete, knowledge of their mother tongue. Besides, arranged marriage issues and strategies seem to have been less imposing on second and third generations, although 'doing it the western way' of knowing the partner fully well prior to marriage, does not go well with their parents.

Bollywood: The Indian Movie Industry

What makes the Indian movie industry so popular not only in India but also amongst the Asian Indian diasporic communities across the globe? While moving to a different country and culture can be intimidating for the immigrant communities, the Indian film industry has had a major role to play in retaining connections with India by creating shared 'cultures of feeling' and a sense of common cultural roots. As Appadurai notes,

> images and values propagated by Bollywood films and picked up in television and advertising filter into the imagination of people living in South Asia and the diaspora, creating thereby a

> 'community of sentiment' that begins to imagine and feel things together.[8]

Additionally, this is one industry that

> titillates their imaginations with fantasies of the 'good life,' defined primarily by the consumption of material goods. These images are interpreted with specificity, particularly in local settings, networks and family relationships that indirectly reinforce fantasies of the affluent West.[9]

It also adds more meaning to the collective dreams, fantasies and an imagination of India of the vast majority of the Asian Indian population, while at the same time enabling them to imagine and romanticize their homeland which would eventually create an urge to visit it. If the western culture enables consumerism and hence 'good life' which fulfill these dreams and fantasies, then

> it also symbolizes wealth, influence and power.[10]

The elaborate song and dance sequences create a world of love and romance, wealth and power for the audience watching individuals who advocate ideal values and emerge victorious.[11] Almost all respondents expressed a close connection with India through Indian movies, which also provided ideas about new forms of clothing and fashion and Indian attires, while also romanticizing India. In a recent study on the concept of identity construction and home amongst the Indian diaspora, Bandhopadhyay found that

> different generations of the Indian diaspora have different reasons for travelling to India. The first generation's nostalgia arises from watching Bollywood movies, and as a result, creates a motivation to travel to India. The second generation's main reason to travel to India is to experience the new 'modern' country, portrayed in the affluent surroundings of contemporary Bollywood movies.[12]

Given the immense popularity of Indian films, both films and video continue to play a significant role in the lives of the Asian Indian community in Ohio, as also elsewhere in America and globally. For it is through these media that the cinematic landscapes become animated while at the same time serving as important

> lenses through which actions and sentiments are understood.[13]

Besides, representing India in beauty pageants in America also draws attention to cultural continuities with India amongst the second generation Asian Indians. In July 2010, Karampal Kaur of Cleveland won the title of Miss USA Punjaban 2010 at a beauty pageant organized by the Punjab Heritage Organization of California. Celebration of India's Independence Day on 15 August 1947, also stirs up an emotional aura amongst the Asian Indians not only in Cleveland but also globally. Thus, while religion, caste, language, marriage are significant institutions that maintain cultural and social ties with India and also define identity, the second generation Asian Indians have successfully managed to negotiate these to form a personal identity that is imbued with varying degrees of being Indian or being American.

Notes

1. Pierre Gittschlich, 2008, 'The Indian Diaspora in the United States of America: An Emerging Political Force?,' in Parvati Raghuram, Ajaya Kumar Shaoo, Brij Maharaj, and Dave Sangha (eds), *Tracing an Indian Diaspora: Contexts, Memories, Representations,* Sage: Los Angeles, 156–70. *Contexts, Memories, Representations.*
2. Surendra K. Gupta, 2004, 'Introduction,' in Surendra K. Gupta (ed.), *Emerging Social Science Concerns: festschrift in honour of Professor Yogesh Atal,* New Delhi: Concept Publishing Company, 1–28, p. 5.
3. Ravinder Barn, 2008, 'Indian Diaspora in the United Kingdom: Second-Generation Parents' Views and Experiences on Heritage

Language Transmission,' in Parvati Raghuram and Ajaya Sahoo et al., *Tracing an Indian Diaspora: Contexts, Memories, Representations*, 191–209, 203.

4. M.N. Srinivas, 1962, *Caste in Modern India and other Essays*, Bombay: Asia Publishing House, 3.
5. John C.B. Webster, 1999, 'Who is a Dalit?,' in S.M. Michael (ed.), *Dalits in Modern India: Vision and Values*, New Delhi: Vistaar Publication, 68.
6. Jyotsna Vaid, 2009, 'Fair Enough? Color and the Commodification of Self in Indian Matrimonials,' in Evelyn Nakano Glenn (ed.), *Shades of Difference: Why Skin Color Matters*, Stanford: Stanford University Press, 148–65, 149.
7. Bhiku Parekh, 1993, 'Some Reflections on the Indian Diaspora,' *Journal of Contemporary Thought*, 3, 105–51.
8. Arjun Appadurai, 1996, *Modernity at Large: Cultural Dimensions of Globalization*, Minneapolis: University of Minnesota Press, 8.
9. Vijay Agnew, 2005, 'Diaspora and Memory,' in Vijay Agnew (ed.), *Diaspora and Memory: A Search for Home*, Toronto: University of Toronto Press, 19–21, 20.
10. Vijay Agnew, 2005, 'Language Matters,' in Vijay Agnew (ed.), *Diaspora and Memory: A Search for Home*, Toronto: University of Toronto Press, 23–47, 33.
11. See Amitav Kumar, 2002, *Bombay-London-New York*, New York: Routledge.
12. Ranjan Bandhopadhyay, December 2008, 'Nostalgia, Identity and Tourism: *Bollywood* in the Indian Diaspora,' *Journal of Tourism and Cultural Change*, 6 (2), 79–100 (abstract).
13. Cynthia J. Miller, 2008, 'Immigrants, Images and Identity: Visualising Homelands Across Borders,' in Parvati Raghuram, Ajaya Kumar Sahoo, Brij Maharaj, Dave Sangha (eds), *Tracing an Indian Diaspora: Contexts, Memories, Representations*, New Delhi: Sage, 284–98, 293.

CHAPTER 5

Understanding the Trajectories of Asian Indians

Concluding Reflections

The first Asian Indians in Cleveland have played a major role in shaping the character of the settlement trajectories following 'dislocation' from India. Having lived for more than four decades in the city, their memories and personal narratives and experiences allude to several formidable challenges faced by them, at the same time managing change and continuity. They presented memories imbued with a lot of sentiments and emotions. For the second generation Asian Indians, these changes exist as new forms of identity, while they in turn looking critically at the position and achievements of an older generation of migrants; made their own decisions about who they are, how they should fit into their new homeland and how they should relate to the land from which their parents, grandparents or even more remote ancestors came.[1]

Although it may be not be feasible to comprehend a site of identification for the second and third generation Asian Indian community in Ohio, there is a sense of displacement from their parents' homeland. Indeed, the Asian Indian community and its presence outside of the parent country, is more of a site offering opportunities for its individual members for expressions and reinterpretations of their cultural beliefs to suit the new spatial locations. These identities are built and rebuilt and expressed by mutual negotiations. The difference, however, is that these negotiations for the first generation Asian Indians are different from the second or third generation members. It is this difference that creates varying levels of conflict between the two and varying levels of perception of the host land and India. Thus, conflict with culture, conflict with parents and the family are common amongst the second and third generation Asian Indians. Thus, the findings of this study offer a range of significant conclusions. The issue of language emerges as a prominent issue amongst the second and third generation Asian Indians in Northeast Ohio, for it is closely intertwined with continuity of cultural identity while adapting to the new social and cultural context. The highlight of language issues is that Hindu Punjabi parents make 'less of an effort' to teach their children Hindi/Punjabi than their Gujarati/South Indian counterparts. While this was recognized by a student, R, my own interactions with Asian Indian parents in Edinburgh and London (UK) revealed the same; the reasons for this attitude are not clear, although it may be that Gujarati and South Indian languages represent specific regions each of which has a culture distinct from the Hindi/Punjabi speaking region of the entire northern and western parts of India. One reason why most second and third generation children are less likely to speak the language of their parents is that although most Asian Indian parents made efforts to speak in their mother tongue, there were limited resources or attempts at 'teaching' them, or even if they did, systemic sources through which this could be continued, did not exist. In any case, raising bilingual children is an onerous task for parents. Besides, there may be an element of preserving language identity, which may also explain the existence of different regional Indian associations in Cleveland, each representing a different cultural unit within the same country of origin, India. This statement is closer to reality than to a mere assumption. The truth is that it also raises new issues on the challenges faced by diasporic parents in transmitting their heritage language to their children.

While language bears a close connection with ethnicity and culture,

> it is generally perceived as a central vehicle for accessing a culture, constructing shared identities and defining out-groups.[2]

Some second generation Asian Indians expressed great difficulty in acquiring the language of their parents when there is little or no extra help to do so.

The study also reveals the paramount significance of a focus on education. In India, education is a passport to successful social status and acceptance. And since most first generation Indians in Ohio immigrated as skilled professionals and educators, they saw the usefulness of education of their children in attaining what they hoped for when they arrived in America. Thus, while cultural and identificational differences may not hamper the overall process of adopting the host country, participation in social, cultural and religious affairs enable adaptation and acculturation of the Asian Indians in Northeast Ohio, as in other parts of America.

On another note, it is also logical to surmise that most of the first generation Asian Indians married within their own caste and religion. The second generation, however, has been flexible on the issue of marriage. While some of them have a white American spouse, others do not wish to follow the traditional marriage norms. Overall, caste and religion play an insignificant role in their lives.

A key issue faced by the first and second generation South Asians is the concerted effort in maintaining a unique identity in a different and new cultural context. The study shows that this has been particularly difficult for the first generation in Cleveland. For them the decision to 'let go' of their cultural values, was far from what they had envisioned before they came to Cleveland. As a result, more emotional energy was spent in 'justifying' and sharing who they were, than in completely accepting the new social challenges they encountered. For the second and third generation Asian Indians, however, 'struggle' is seen in terms of maintaining a new identity in America – an identity that sometimes is at odds with that of the earlier generation. Whilst they recognize their 'Indian' identity and cultural roots through their parents, a majority have been able to construct their own identity as part of their life in America. But these are issues that South Asians will face as a result of generational differences. All in all, continuous struggle to maintain an 'identity' is inevitable in all diasporic communities, not only in America but globally.

An important highlight of the study is that the first generation of Indian women achieved a new sense of selfhood and autonomy, as physician, teacher or a social worker. This was especially laudable at a time when gender restrictions in India could not be easily avoided. Autonomy for these women, thus, meant education and professional advancement.[3] Almost all women respondents in this study migrated to America with their husbands than to fulfill their educational or professional aspirations. Often marked by 'pangs of dislocation' and 'hopes of a new beginning,'[4] the initial dependence, especially of educated and professional women, thus,

> creates many complex, material and emotional problems that may not be foreseen prior to emigration because of preconceived utopian notions of the receiving society.[5]

While memory and a collective consciousness of a 'lost homeland' are explicitly expressed in terms of reconstructed and institutionalized cultural thoughts which relate to India to which the first Asian Indians, at least, are committed and to which they hope to return to, it works differently for the second generation. The latter, closely identifying themselves with the American culture, maintain functional links with India, expressed through the film and entertainment industry, food, music and traditional costumes and festivities.

It is ironic that although there may be a general non-acceptability of Indian traditions as in gendered roles, system of joint family and certain religious customs in practice, the Asian Indian community connects with its parent country through the ideals of the popular and the largest film industry in the world, Bollywood (the Indian film industry). The immense popularity of Hindi language in the film industry makes them one of the most significant cultural forms in national and transnational South Asian cultural practices.[6] Thus, Indian films provide a medium and images through which the Indian communities engage and share the same set of social and cultural values. For these images and values that pervade popular culture, play a role in constructing the dreams and fantasies of people living in different locations.[7] The regional TV satellite channels broadcasting Bollywood dramas and soap operas still offer a pursuit for relaxation for Indian communities of all age groups. While music and films have played a significant and indispensable role in maintaining important connections with the homeland, they have also acted as a medium of a strong 'cultural flow.'[8]

The Sikh community in America, Britain and Canada has also played a major role in the political, economic and social life of Punjab in India. This will be an interesting area for future research, especially on the manner in which they have kept the cultural exchange through exchange of ideas, visits and pilgrimages, all of which have contributed to legitimation of Sikh social and cultural aspirations. The Sikh 'Dewans' have established links with several Sikh organizations globally which also paves the way for a fresh look at new ways of understanding the Sikh past.

The experiences of the first Asian Indians in Cleveland, are more than a construction of the 'selves' and of identities. They represent a framework within which larger social issues of race, ethnicity and plural cultures in a global context can be understood. As 'never heard or documented before', the views of the second and third generation Indians in Northeast Ohio, on the other hand, call for understanding issues of identity dilemmas in a different cultural context.

It is time that we initiate a dialogue on the dynamics of cultural creation of identity or multiple identities amongst various communities in Cleveland. In view of this, much remains to be said about engagements of the Sikh community in 'social service' activities in Cleveland, as also in other regions, which calls for more focused studies on their lives and contributions to the global world. Besides, issues of religious and cultural representations also bring to fore questions on the maintenance or rejection of religious practices amongst the subsequent generations of Asian Indians. Equally significant is the manner in which the subsequent generations of Asian Indians, born in America, express and negotiate their ethnic identity in various contexts,[9] often created through the realm of consumption.[10]

To conclude, this study throws light on the significant trajectory of integration of Asian Indians in Northeast Ohio – a trajectory that was long, successful and sometimes difficult, but could never be impeded by new socio-cultural contexts; a trajectory which despite the initial odds, has

> both intensified and legitimated virtually an Indian immigrant's ongoing engagement with India as well as India's own outreach to its diaspora.[11]

Ghosh[12] labels this engagement as an 'epic relationship' of imagination and not the relationship through religion or politics or culture; for Ghosh, it is the former that usefully links India with her diasporic communities globally. However, despite varying perceptions of the Asian Indian community, I hope that this study has been successful in giving a voice, representation and social visibility to the Asian Indian community in Northeast Ohio in a historical and social space that has inspired them to follow the four '**A**'s of cultural assimilation and change. All in all, the study was undertaken on a small scale to understand and unravel personal trajectories in the hope to inspiring and eliciting further interest in learning about the travails of the Asian Indian community with a much wider scope and in a global context.

Notes

1. Judith M. Brown, 2006, *Global South Asians: Introducing the Modern Diaspora*, Cambridge: Cambridge University Press, 28–9.
2. Ravinder Barn, 2008, 'Indian Diaspora in the United Kingdom: Second-Generation Parents' Views and Experiences on Heritage Language Transmission,' in Parvati Raghuram and Ajaya Sahoo, et al. (eds), *Tracing an Indian Diaspora: Contexts, Memories, Representations*, New Delhi: Sage, 191–209, 203.
3. See Aparna Sircar, 2000, *Work Roles, Gender roles, and Asian Indian Immigrant Women in the United States*, New York: The Edwin Mellen Press, 26–52.

4. Mala Pandurang, 2008, 'Moving Beyond, Moving Ahead: Possible Paradigms for Accessing Indian Emigrant Subjectivities,' in Parvati Raghuram and Ajaya Sahoo, et al. (eds), *Tracing an Indian Diaspora: Contexts, Memories, Representations*, New Delhi: Sage 271–283, 277.
5. Mala Pandurang, ibid.
6. Jigna Desai, 2004, *Beyond Bollywood: The Cultural Politics of South Asian Diasporic Film*, New York: Routledge, 35.
7. See Jigna Desai, ibid.
8. Tony Ballantyne, 2007, 'Introduction,' in Tony Ballantyne, *Textures of the Sikh Past: New Historical Perspectives*, Oxford: Oxford University Press, 1–16,12.
9. See also Geoffrey Burkhart, 2008, 'Identity Dilemmas: Gay South Asian men in North America,' in Parvati Raghuram Ajaya Sahoo et al. (eds), *Tracing an Indian Diaspora: Contexts, Memories, Representations*, New Delhi: Sage, 299–319, 308.
10. For details, see M. Khandelwal, 1995, 'Indian Immigrants in Queens, New York City: Patterns of Spatial Concentration and Distribution 1965–1990,' in Peter van der Veer (ed.), *Nation and Migration: The Politics of Space in the South Asian Diaspora*, Philadelphia: University of Pennsylvania Press.
11. Johanna Lessinger, 2002, 'Indian Immigrants in the United States: the Emergence of a Transnational Population,' in Bhiku Parekh, Gurharpal Singh and Steven Vertovec (eds), *Culture and Economy in the Indian Diaspora* , London and New York: Routledge, 165–82, 179.
12. For details, see Amitav Ghosh, 1989, 'The Diaspora in Indian Culture,' *Public Culture*, 2 (1): 73–8, 76.

Bibliography

Agnew, Vijay (ed.). 2005. *Diaspora, Memory, and Identity: A Search for Home*, Toronto: University of Toronto Press.

——2005. 'Diaspora and Memory' in Vijay Agnew (ed.), *Diaspora and Memory: Search for Home*, Toronto: University of Toronto Press, 19–21.

——2005. 'Language Matters' in Vijay Agnew (ed.), *Diaspora and Memory: Search for Home*, Toronto, University of Toronto Press, 23–47.

Altshuler, Nathan et al. (eds), *Migration and Modernization: The Indian Diaspora in Comparative Perspective* (Studies in Third World Societies), 13–23.

Appadurai, Arjun. 1996. *Modernity at Large: Cultural Dimensions of Globalization*, Minneapolis: University of Minnesota Press.

Ashcroft, Bill, Gareth Griffiths and Helen Tiffin (eds). 1989. *The Empire Writes Back*, London: Routledge.

Bala, Poonam (October) 2013. 'Asian Indians: Significant Highlights of the Community in Northeast Ohio,' *The Encyclopedia of Cleveland History*, Cleveland.

Ballantyne, Tony. 2007. 'Introduction,' in Tony Ballantyne, *Textures of the Sikh Past: New Historical Perspectives*, Oxford: Oxford University Press, 1–16.

Bandhopadhyay, Ranjan. (December) 2008. 'Nostalgia, Identity and Tourism: Bollywood in the Indian Diaspora,' *Journal of Tourism and Cultural Changes*, 6 (2), 79–100 (Abstract).

Barn, Ravinder. 2008. 'Indian Diaspora in the United Kingdom: Second Generation Parents' Views and Experiences on Heritage Language Transmission,' in Parvati Raghuram, Ajaya Sahoo et al. (eds), *Tracing an Indian Diaspora: Contexts, Memories, Representations*, New Delhi: Sage, 191–209.

Baubock, Rainer and Thoams Faist (eds). 2010. *Diaspora and Transnationalism: Concepts, Theories and Methods*, IMISCOE Research: Amsterdam University Press.

Brown, Judith M. 2006. *Global South Asians: Introducing the Modern Diaspora*, Cambridge: Cambridge University Press.

Burkhart, Geoffrey. 2008. 'Identity Dilemmas: Gay South Asian Men in North America,' in Parvati Raghuram, Ajaya Sahoo et al. (eds), *Tracing an Indian Diaspora: Contexts, Memories, Representations*, New Delhi: Sage, 299–319.

Chaliand, G. (ed.). 1998. *Minority Peoples in the Age of Nation-States*. London: Pluto.

Chand, Tara. 1992. *The History of the Freedom Movement in India*, Delhi: Ministry of Information and Broadcasting (Government of India), V 3.

Cleveland Ethnic Directory, 1990, Nationalities Services Center: Cleveland.

Desai, Jigna. 2004. *Beyond Bollywood: The Cultural Politics of South Asian Diasporic Film*, New York: Routledge, 35.

Diesel, Alleyn. 2003. 'Hinduism in KwaZulu-Natal, South Africa' in Bhiku Parekh, Gurharpal Singh and Steven Vertovec, *Culture and Economy in the Indian Diaspora*, London: Routledge, 33–50.

Divakaruni, Chitra Banerjee. 2001. *Arranged Marriages: Stories*, New York: Anchor Books, 1995.

Faist, Thomas. 2000. *The Volume and Dynamics of International Migration and Transnational Social Spaces*, Oxford: Oxford University Press.

Fanon, Frantz. 1963. 'On National Culture,' in Frantz Fanon, *The Wretched of the Earth* (trans. by Richard Philcox), New York: Grove Press.

Federation of India Community Associations (FICA). 2006–07. 'What our Indian-ness Offers the World,' Annual Report, (Cleveland: Federation of Indian Community Associations of NE Ohio).

Fugita, Stephen, David Namkoong, Domingo Patawarn, and Suey Yee. 1977. Asian Americans and their Communities of Cleveland, Cleveland State University: Cleveland.

Gall, Susan B. and Gall, Timothy L. (eds). 1993. *Statistical Record of Asian Americans*, Detroit: Gale Research Inc.

Ghai, Dharam P. and Yash. P Ghai. 1965. 'Asians in East Africa: Problems and Prospects,' *The Journal of Modern African Studies*, 3, 35–51.

Giridharadas, Anand. 2011. *India Calling: An Intimate Portrait of a Nation's Remaking*, New York: Henry Holt and Company.

Gittschlich, Pierre. 2008. 'The Indian Diaspora in the United States of America: An Emerging Political Force?' in Parvati Raghuram, Ajaya Kumar Shaoo, Brij Maharaj, and Dave Sangha (eds). *Tracing an Indian Diaspora: Contexts, Memories, Representations*, New Delhi: Sage, 156–70.

Glazer, Nathan and Patrick Moynihan (eds). 1963. *Beyond the Melting Pot: The Negroes, Puerto Ricans, Jews, Italians and Irish of New York City*, Cambridge, MA: MIT Press.

Glenn, Evelyn Nakano (ed.). 2009. *Shades of Difference: Why Skin Color Matters*, Stanford: Stanford University Press.

Grabowski, John J. and Diane Ewart Grabowski. 2000. *Cleveland: A History in Motion*, California: Heritage Media Corporation.

Gupta, Surendra. 2004. 'Introduction,' in Surendra Gupta (ed.), *Emerging Social Science Concerns: Festschrift in Honour of Professor Yogesh Atal*, New Delhi: Concept Publishing Company, 1–28.

Hall, Stuart. 1990. 'Cultural Identity and Diaspora' in J. Rutherford (ed.), *Identity, Community, Culture and Difference*, London: Lawrence and Wishart.

Iosifides, Theodoros. 2011. *Qualitative Methods in Migration Studies: A Critical Realist Perspective*, Surrey: Ashgate Publishing Limited.

Isaksen, Leonard Karen. 1997. *The South Asian Americans*, Westport: Greenwood Press.

Jacobsen, Knut A. and P. Pratap Kumar (eds).2004. *South Asians in the Diaspora: Histories and Religious Traditions*, Leiden: Brill.

Jain, Shobita. 2010. 'Trans-migrant Women's Agency and Indian Diaspora,' *South Asian Diaspora*, 2 (2), 185–200.

Jensen, J.M. 1988, *Passage from India: Asian Indian Immigrant in North America*, New Haven, CT: Yale University Press.

Khandelwal, M. 1995. 'Indian Immigrants in Queens, New York City: Patterns of Spatial Concentration and Distribution 1965–1990,' in Peter van der Veer (ed.), *Nation and Migration: The Politics of Space in the South Asian Diaspora*, Philadelphia: University of Pennsylvania Press.

Kumar, Amitav, 2002. *Bombay-London-New York*, New York: Routledge.

Kundu, Amitabh. 2009 (June). 'Urbanisation and Migration: An Analysis of Trends, Patterns and Policies in Asia,' UNDP (Human Development Reports) Research Paper.

Kuper, H. 1960. *Indian People in Natal*, Pietermaritzburg: University of Natal Press.

Lessinger, Johanna. 2005. 'Indian Immigrants in the United States: The Emergence of a Transnational Population' in Bhiku Parekh, Gurharpal Singh and Steven Vertovec (eds), *Culture and Economy in the Indian Diaspora*, London and New York: Routledge, 165–82.

Lindberg, Anna. 2004. 'Transformation of Marriage Patterns in the Kerala Diaspora in the U.S.' in Knut A. Jacobsen and Pratap Kumar (eds), *South Asians in the Diaspora: Histories and Religious Traditions*, Leiden: Brill, 203–219.

Marienstrass, R. 1998. 'On the Notion of Diaspora' in G. Chaliand (ed.) *Minority Peoples in the Age of Nation-States*. London: Pluto, 119–125.

Michael, S.M. (ed.). 1999. *Dalits in Modern India: Vision and Values*, New Delhi: Vistaar Publication.

Miller, Cynthia J. 2008. 'Immigrants, Images and Identity: Visualising Homelands Across Borders,' in Parvati Raghuram, Ajaya Kumar Sahoo (eds), *Tracing an Indian Diaspora: Contexts, Memories and Representations*, New Delhi: Sage, 284–98.

Narayan, Kirin. 2004. 'Haunting Stories: Narrative Transmissions and South Asian Diaspora' in Knut A. Jacobsen and P. Pratap Kumar (eds), *South Asians in the Diaspora: Histories and Religious Traditions*, Leiden: Brill, 415–34.

Pandurang, Mala. 2008. 'Moving Beyond, Moving Ahead: Possible Paradigms for Accessing Indian Emigrant Subjectivities,' in Parvati Raghuram and Ajaya Sahoo, et al. (eds), *Tracing an Indian Diaspora: Contexts, Memories, Representations*, New Delhi: Sage 271–83.

Parekh, Bhiku, Gurharpal Singh and Steven Vertovec (eds). 2005. *Culture and Economy in the Indian Diaspora*, London and New York: Routledge.

Parekh, Bhiku. 1993. 'Some Reflections on the Indian Diaspora,' *Journal of Contemporary Thought*, 3, 105–51.

Raghuram, Parvati and Ajay Kumar Sahoo et al. (eds). 2008. *Tracing an Indian Diaspora: Contexts, Memories, Representations*, New Delhi: Sage.

Raghuram, Parvati and Ajay Kumar Sahoo. 2008. "Thinking 'Indian Diaspora' for Our Times" in Parvati Raghuram and Ajay Kumar Sahoo et al. (eds). *Tracing an Indian Diaspora: Contexts, Memories, Representations*, New Delhi: Sage, 1–20.

Raumann, Martin. 2004. 'Becoming a Colour of the Rainbow: Social Integration of Indian Hindus in Trinidad, Analysed Along a Phase Model of Diaspora' in Knut A.Jacobsen and P.Pratap Kumar (eds), *South Asians in the Diaspora: Histories and Religious Traditions*, Leiden: Brill, 77–96.

Sahay, Anjali. 2009. *Indian Diaspora in the United States: Brain Drain or Gain?*, Lanham: Lexington Books.

Said, E. 2005. 'Out of Place: A Memoir, London: Granta' in Alison Blunt, *Domicile and Diaspora: Anglo-Indian Women and the Spatial Politics of Home*, Massachussetts: Blackwell Publishing.

Sen, Amartya. 2005. *The Argumentative Indian: Writings on Indian History, Culture and Identity*, London: Allen Lane.

Shukla, Sandhya. 2003. *India Abroad: Diasporic Cultures of Postwar America and England*, New Jersey: Princeton University Press.

Shuval, Judith T. 2000. 'Diaspora Migration: Definitional Ambiguities and a Theoretical Paradigm,' *International Migration*, 38(5): 41–56.

Singh, Gurharpal. 2003. 'Introduction,' in *Culture and Economy in the Indian Diaspora*, Bhikhu Parekh, Gurharpal Singh, and Steven Vertovec (eds), London: Routledge, 1–12.

Sircar, Aparna. 2000. *Work Role, Gender Roles and Asian Indian Immigrant Women in the United States*, Lewison, NY: The Edwin Mellen Press.

Sokefeld, Martin. 2000. 'Religion or Culture? Concepts of Identity in the Alevi Diaspora,' Paper presented at a Conference on Locality, Identity, Diaspora, University of Hamburg.

Sood, Ajeet Singh. 17 May 1965. *The Cleveland Press*, Cleveland.

Srinivas, M.N. 1962. *Caste in Modern India and other Essays*, Bombay: Asia Publishing House.

Sugiman, Pamela. 2005. 'Memories of Internment: Narrating Japanese-Canadian Women's Life's Stories' in Vijay Agnew (ed.), *Diaspora, Memory, and Identity: A Search for Home*, Toronto: University of Toronto Press, 48–77.

Sutlive, Vinson H. and Nathan Altshuler et al (eds). 1981. *Migration and Modernization: The Indian Diaspora in Comparative Perspective* (Studies in Third World Societies, Williamsburg, VA).

The Encyclopedia of Cleveland History. (October) 2013, Cleveland. *The Lotus*, March 1968 (6).

Tololyan, Khachig 1991. The Nation State and its Others: In Lieu of a Preface. *Diaspora*, 1 (1), 3–7.

Vaid, Jyotsna. 2009. 'Fair' Enough? Color and the Commodification of Self in Indian Matrimonials,' in Evelyn Nakano Glenn (ed.), *Shades of Difference: Why Skin Color Matters*, Stanford: Stanford University Press, 148–165.

Van der Veer, Peter (ed.). 1995. *Nation and Migration: The Politics of Space in the South Asian Diaspora*, Philadelphia: University of Pennsylvania Press.

Van Tassel, David D. and John J. Grabowski, 1987 and 1996. *The Encyclopedia of Cleveland History*, Bloomington: Indian University Press.

Varadarajan, Latha. 2010. *The Domestic Abroad: Diasporas in International Relations*, Oxford: Oxford University Press.

Waddell, Charles E. and Glenn M. Vernon. 1981. 'Ethnic Identity and National Identification: The Social Construction of Commitment of Indian Immigrants to Australia,' in Vinson H. Sutlive and Nathan Altshuler et al. (eds), *Migration and Modernization: The Indian Diaspora in Comparative Perspective* (Studies in Third World Societies).

Webster, John C.B. 1999. 'Who is a Dalit?' in S.M. Michael (ed.), *Dalits in Modern India: Vision and Values*, New Delhi: Vistaar Publication, 68–79.

Appendix

india
association
of cleveland
For the Advancement of the Indian Community

CONSTITUTION

(This Constitution was adopted and ratified in April 1964, and amended in December 1968, August 1969, February 1972, October 1972 and September 1973).

ARTICLE I Name and Objectives

Section 1 The name of the Association shall be India Association of Cleveland.

Section 2 The objectives of the Association shall be to educate, promote and present a clear picture of Indian traditions, customs and recent Indian developments to the people of Cleveland, Ohio; to arrange for the celebration of Indian national holidays, foster closer ties among the Indians in Cleveland, Ohio, and to promote friendship and cultural exchange with other Associations, organizations and groups, foreign and American, in Ohio.

ARTICLE II Membership

Section 1 Membership in the Association shall be of three classes:

a) Regular members

b) Associate Members

c) Honorary Members

Section 2 a) Regular Members: These shall be any Indian citizens over the age of 16 who are interested in the objectives of the Association.

b) Associate Members: These shall be non-Indians above the age of 16 who are interested in the objectives of the Association.

c) Honorary Members: These shall be nominated by the Executive Board of the Association. Such members are not required to be Indian citizens.

Section 3 Annual dues shall be: $4.00 per year for single members; $6.00 per year for married couples. No dues shall be required of Honorary Members. (As amended in September 1973)

ARTICLE III Officers of Executive Board

Section 1 The Officers of the Association shall be a President, Vice President, Treasurer, Secretary, Joint Secretary and four Committee members, all of whom shall comprise the Executive Board of nine.

Section 2 The Officers shall be elected once a year at the Annual Meeting of the Association Membership which shall be held in the month of February.

Section 3 No member shall be eligible to contest for election to the same office for more than two times consecutively.

Section 4 The President shall be an ex officio member of all committees.

Section 5 The outgoing President shall be requested to serve as an ex officio member of the Executive Board, for six months following the completion of his or her term of office.

Section 6 An Officer wishing to resign from his or her position shall give a three-week notice and confirm it in writing to the Executive Board. (As passed in August 1969)

Section 7 Vacancies shall be filled by nominations rendered by the Officers and approved by the Executive Board, subject to final ratification by the Membership in its next meeting.

Section 8 The Editor of "The Lotus" will attend all the executive committee meetings but will have no voting right in these meetings. The treasurer of IAC will also be the treasurer of the Lotus board. (As amended in February 1972)

ARTICLE IV Election Procedures

Section 1 All members shall have a right to vote and to contest for the election of the officers. Associate members and Honorary members shall not have such rights.

Section 2 Nine members shall be elected to the Executive Board by the Membership. All nominees for the President, at the time of election, must be members of the newly elected Executive Board. The President shall be elected by the Membership. The Executive Board shall elect other Officers from its remaining members of the newly elected body. (As amended in August 1969)

Section 3 The elections shall be conducted by secret ballot, and simple majority shall govern.

Section 4 Other detailed procedures for the elections shall be determined by the Executive Board.

ARTICLE V Meetings

Section 1 All meetings shall be called by the Secretary in consultation with the President and in his absence, in consultation with the Vice President.

Section 2 Regular meetings of the Executive Board shall be held once a month on the first Sunday when feasible.

Section 3 Emergency meetings of the Board shall be called whenever necessary.

Section 4 The quorum for a meeting of the Executive Board shall be two-thirds of the strength of the regular Board.

Section 5 The membership shall meet at least twice a year including the annual election meeting, on being convened by the Executive Board.

The Executive Board, if it deems necessary, shall convene an Emergency Meeting of the Membership, to discuss any special issue which needs urgent consideration.

Notice of the Membership meet shall be mailed to the members two weeks in advance of the meeting, except that, in case of an emergency meeting, this duration is not deemed necessary. (As amended in August 1969)

Section 6 Quorum necessary for the all membership meeting including emergency meetings, but excluding the annual election meeting, shall be ten percentage (10%) of the dues paid members of the association for that fiscal year. The quorum necessary for the annual election meeting will be twenty-five percentage (25%) of the dues paid members of the association for that fiscal year. (As amended in February 1972)

Section 7 A membership meeting may be petitioned by one-third of the regular dues paid members in writing filed with the Secretary and the President of the Association.

Section 8 All Executive Board and membership meetings shall be chaired by the President, in whose absence the Vice President shall assume his responsibilities. After them, the order of succession will be Secretary, Joint Secretary and Treasurer.

ARTICLE VI Finances

Section 1 The Association shall keep its funds in a bank. The Executive Board shall, by resolution, designate one or more Officers to sign checks on said bank account of the Association. Funds of the Association may be used only to further the objectives of the Association.

Section 2 An Auditor shall be elected by the general body according to Article IV, Section 3 of the Constitution. He shall be an ex officio member of the Executive Board and therefore shall be non-voting. He shall have an access to all the financial records of the Association. He must certify the books as correct by countersigning the Treasurer's Report. The Auditor shall serve for one full year beginning with the election in the month of February. (As passed in August 1969)

Section 3 The Treasurer shall pay expenses only for which receipts are provided, unless expressly authorized to do otherwise by the Executive Board. He shall be obliged to keep books in a regular manner which shall be open to the inspection of the Auditor. Any expenditure over ten dollars must be authorized in advance either by the Treasurer or the Executive Board. (As passed in August 1969)

Section 4 Should the Association disband, the entire assets of the Association shall be transferred to the

Indian Embassy in Washington, D.C. to be used by said Embassy as it deems fit.

ARTICLE VII Membership Obligations

Section 1 All members of the India Association shall strive to fulfill the aims and objectives of the Association, and shall not indulge in any activities detrimental to the honor and prestige of India, the Indian community or the India Association. (As passed in August 1969)

Section 2 No member or group of members of the Association shall initiate or continue any activity or activities in the name of the Indian community or the India Association, without the prior approval of the Executive Board. The Executive Board is answerable to the Membership in dealing with such a situation, and if it deems necessary, shall call an Emergency membership Meeting to discuss and decide any matter arising in this connection, including the guiding principles, and the relationship of such activity or activities within the framework of the India Association. (As passed in August 1969)

Section 3 All efforts of the members toward any of the Association activities shall be considered voluntary. No compensation shall be paid to any member for the labor donated. Members can be compensated only for the out-of-pocket expenses incurred by them for the Association activities in accordance with Section 3, Article VI (Finances) of the Constitution. The definition of "member" under this section shall include the children of the active members of the Association. (As amended in October 1972)

ARTICLE VIII Disciplinary Action

Section 1 Any member or group of members indulging in any activity in contravention of Article VII, or responsible for any impropriety or misconduct, shall be liable to disciplinary action which shall be decided by the Membership. (As passed in August 1969)

Section 2 In case of any impropriety on the part of any member of the Executive Board, excluding the President, the Executive Board shall have the right to dismiss that member by at least five votes of the Executive Board.

Section 3 An Officer that remains absent for two consecutive meetings of the Executive Board, for no legitimate reason, shall be considered expelled from his or her office on the Board. (As passed in August 1969)

Section 4 In case of any impropriety on the part of the President, the matter shall be placed before the Membership. Such meetings may be called by the Secretary in consultation with the Vice President.

ARTICLE IX Radio Program

The Executive Board shall appoint a Committee to continue the Radio Program. This Committee shall consist of a Program Director, a Script Writer, a Business Manager, and one or more Announcers. (As passed in February 1970)

ARTICLE X India House Project

IAC shall seek the establishment of a center designated "INDIA HOUSE", in Cleveland, to further the objectives of the Association. The Executive Board shall set aside an amount of $ 1.00 for every single membership, and $ 2.00 from every family membership towards this project.

A separate Board of Governors consisting of six members of IAC, to be elected by the general body at the annual elections, shall govern this project. Each member of the Board of Governors shall be elected for a period of three years. Two members of this Board will be up for re-election every year. President of IAC shall be an ex officio member of the Board of Governors. (As passed in September 1973)

ARTICLE XI Revision

Section 1 These by-laws may be modified or amended by majority vote by the Membership, if prior notice is mailed to members two weeks in advance of the meeting.

ARTICLE XII Interpretation and Definitions

Section 1 The decision of at least five members of the Executive Board including the President on any question involving the interpretation of these by-laws and any definitions required therein, shall be final.

india
association
of cleveland
For the Advancement of the Indian Community

<u>IF YOU HAVE FILLED THIS QUESTIONNAIRE ONCE, PLEASE DON'T FILL IT AGAIN</u>

Dear Member:

The Indian population in Greater Cleveland has increased more than ten fold during the sixties. As a result, the India Association of Cleveland came into being in 1964, The constitution of IAC was modified in 1970 (further modified in 1973) to give the Indian community a permanent identity by establishing an INDIA HOUSE, which will serve the community and other interested residents in Cleveland. In order to make further progress, we need to get your ideas and suggestions and would appreciate your filling out this form. Your may either send it by mail to the address indicated or drop it off in a box at the movies.

Thank you very much.

L. N. Sampath

Questionnaire for India House

1. Do you agree with the idea of establishing a more permanent form of identity for the Indian community?

   ☐ yes ☐ No

2. Do you agree that India House will give us that permanent identity?

   ☐ yes ☐ No

3. What preference do you have as far as location of India House is concerned? (Write numbers 1 to 4 in the squares below indicating your order of choice)

☐ Case Western Reserve Univ.

☐ Downtown or Cleveland State University

☐ Suburb

☐ Other Specify ________________

4. What type of facilities should be available at India House? (Show preference by using 1 to 8 numbers in the squares)

☐ Information Service ☐ Lodging

☐ Period Special Programs ☐ Meetings

☐ Recreation ☐ Library

☐ Boarding

☐ Others, Please specify ________________________

5. If there was an India House, how often and when would you and your family use it?

☐ Everyday ☐ Twice a week

☐ Once a Week ☐ Once a month

☐ Weekends ☐ Never

☐ Other, Please specify ___________________

6. What time of the day do you think you will use India House facilities?

☐ Mornings ☐ Evenings ☐ Day

7. Would you bring your American friends to India House?

☐ Yes ☐ No

8. Should the India House be exclusively used by the India Association of Cleveland or rented to other organizations or individuals?

   ☐ Exclusively by IAC ☐ Rent it to others

9. This ambitious program is going to require funds and concerted effort by the Indian community. Please check the ways in which you will be able to help. (Your donations will be tax-exempt.)

   ☐ I will donate $100 for charter membership.

   ☐ I will donate $500 for trusteeship.

   ☐ I will donate $1000 for life membership.

   ☐ I will donate $ ________________

   ☐ I will help in raising funds by ______________

10. Any other comments ______________________________

    ______________________ ___________________________

11. Name ____

    Company affiliation ______________________________

    Address ____

    Phone: Res. ________________ Office ______________

Mail to: P.O. Box 5206, Cleveland, Ohio 44101

January, 1974

Index